Coding Basics with Microsoft Visual Studio

Kiet Huynh

Table of Contents

CHAPTER I
Introduction to Coding and Microsoft Visual Studio

1.1 Understanding the Basics of Coding

In today's digital age, coding has become an essential skill, powering the technology that surrounds us. From websites and mobile apps to software applications and IoT devices, coding is the language that makes it all possible. This chapter serves as your stepping stone into the world of coding, providing a solid foundation for your journey with Microsoft Visual Studio.

What is Coding?

Coding, also known as programming, is the process of creating instructions that a computer can understand and execute. These instructions, written in programming languages, dictate how software and applications function. Coding enables you to turn your ideas into tangible solutions, from simple scripts to complex software systems.

Why Learn Coding?

Learning coding opens up a world of opportunities. It nurtures problem-solving skills, logical thinking, and creativity. It empowers you to innovate, automate tasks, and create tools that streamline everyday processes. With coding skills, you can contribute to various industries, from healthcare to entertainment, by developing solutions that address real-world challenges.

Introduction to Microsoft Visual Studio

Microsoft Visual Studio is a powerful integrated development environment (IDE) that simplifies the coding process. It provides a suite of tools, features, and resources to help you write, edit, debug, and deploy code efficiently. Whether you're a beginner or an experienced developer, Visual Studio offers a user-friendly interface to enhance your coding experience.

Navigating the Visual Studio Interface

Let's take a brief tour of the Visual Studio interface to familiarize ourselves with its key components:

1. Menu Bar: The topmost bar contains various menus, including File, Edit, View, and more. These menus offer access to different functions and commands.

2. Toolbar: Just below the menu bar, you'll find the toolbar with icons that represent frequently used actions like opening files, saving, and running code.

3. Solution Explorer: On the right-hand side, the Solution Explorer displays your projects, files, and folders in a hierarchical structure.

4. Code Editor: The main area in the center is the code editor, where you write and edit your code. Visual Studio provides syntax highlighting, code completion, and debugging features to assist you.

5. Output Window: The bottom section houses the Output window, where you can view build and debug outputs, messages, and errors.

6. Tool Windows: Visual Studio offers various tool windows like Properties, Team Explorer, and Error List, which provide context-specific information and options.

Getting Started with Your First Code

Let's kick off your coding journey with a simple example using Microsoft Visual Studio:

1. Launch Visual Studio: Open Microsoft Visual Studio on your computer. You can find it in the Start menu or by searching for it.

2. Create a New Project: Click on "File" > "New" > "Project..." Select a programming language, such as C# or Python, and choose a project template, like "Console Application."

3. Write Your Code: In the code editor, you'll see a basic template. Write a simple program, such as displaying "Hello, World!" on the screen.

4. Run Your Code: Click on the "Run" button (usually a green triangle icon) on the toolbar. You'll see the output of your program in the Output window.

Congratulations! You've written and executed your first code using Microsoft Visual Studio. This is just the beginning of your coding journey, and Visual Studio will be your

1.2. Overview of Microsoft Visual Studio

Microsoft Visual Studio is a comprehensive integrated development environment (IDE) that caters to a wide range of programming languages and application types. It offers a suite of tools and features designed to simplify the coding process, enhance productivity, and enable developers to build high-quality software applications. In this section, we will delve deeper into the key features and functionalities of Microsoft Visual Studio.

Key Features of Microsoft Visual Studio:

1. Multi-Language Support: Visual Studio supports an array of programming languages, including C#, Python, JavaScript, Java, and more. This versatility allows developers to work on diverse projects without switching between different IDEs.

2. Code Editing and Navigation: The code editor in Visual Studio provides intelligent code completion, syntax highlighting, and automatic error checking. Developers can navigate through their codebase easily using features like Go to Definition and Find All References.

3. Integrated Debugger: Visual Studio's built-in debugger helps developers identify and fix errors in their code. It allows setting breakpoints, inspecting variables, and stepping through code execution to track down bugs.

4. Project Templates: The IDE offers a variety of project templates that serve as starting points for different types of applications. Whether you're creating a web app, mobile app, desktop software, or game, Visual Studio has you covered.

5. Version Control: Visual Studio seamlessly integrates with version control systems like Git and Azure DevOps, enabling efficient collaboration among team members and effective code management.

6. Extensions and Add-ons: The Visual Studio Marketplace hosts a plethora of extensions and add-ons that enhance the IDE's capabilities. Developers can install extensions for additional language support, tools, and integrations.

7. Application Deployment: Visual Studio facilitates easy deployment of applications to various platforms, including web servers, app stores, and cloud services. It provides configuration wizards and deployment options to streamline the process.

8. Performance Profiling: Developers can use performance profiling tools to analyze and optimize the performance of their applications. These tools help identify bottlenecks and improve the overall efficiency of the code.

9. Cloud Integration: Visual Studio offers seamless integration with Microsoft Azure, allowing developers to build, deploy, and manage cloud-based applications directly from the IDE.

Getting Started with Microsoft Visual Studio:

To get started with Microsoft Visual Studio, follow these steps:

1. Installation: Download and install Microsoft Visual Studio from the official website. Choose the version that best suits your needs, such as Visual Studio Community, Professional, or Enterprise.

2. Launching Visual Studio: Once installed, launch the IDE. You will be greeted with a start page where you can create a new project, open an existing project, or explore recent projects.

3. Creating a New Project: Click on "Create a new project" to open the project templates window. Select the desired project type, programming language, and template. For instance, you can choose "ASP.NET Core Web Application" if you're creating a web app using ASP.NET Core.

4. Coding: The selected project template will provide you with a basic project structure and initial code. Begin coding in the code editor, and take advantage of features like code completion and error checking.

5. Building and Running: Once you've written your code, build the project by clicking on the "Build" button. To run the application, click on the "Run" button. You can also debug your code using breakpoints and the integrated debugger.

By familiarizing yourself with Microsoft Visual Studio's features and capabilities, you'll be better equipped to embark on your coding journey and create impactful software applications. As you delve deeper into coding, you'll uncover the full potential of this versatile IDE and harness its tools to bring your coding projects to life.

1.3 Setting Up Your Development Environment

Setting up your development environment is a crucial step in getting started with coding using Microsoft Visual Studio. A well-configured environment ensures a smooth coding experience and enables you to take full advantage of Visual Studio's features. In this section, we will walk you through the process of setting up your development environment.

Step-by-Step Guide to Setting Up Your Development Environment:

1. Install Microsoft Visual Studio: If you haven't already, download and install Microsoft Visual Studio from the official website. Choose the edition that suits your needs, such as Visual Studio Community, Professional, or Enterprise. Follow the installation prompts to complete the setup.

2. Select Workloads: During the installation, you'll be prompted to select workloads based on the type of applications you intend to develop. Workloads include options like ".NET desktop development," "ASP.NET and web development," "Python development," and more. Choose the workloads that align with your coding goals.

3. Install Additional Components: After selecting workloads, you can choose to install additional components such as language packs, SDKs, and tools. These components enhance your development capabilities and support different programming languages.

4. Configure Visual Studio Settings: Once Visual Studio is installed, open the IDE. You can customize the appearance and behavior of Visual Studio by configuring settings. Access settings through the "Tools" menu and explore options related to themes, fonts, code formatting, and keybindings. Adjust these settings to match your preferences.

5. Create a New Project: To begin coding, create a new project by clicking on "Create a new project" on the start page. Select a project template that corresponds to the type of application you want to build. For instance, if you're creating a C# console application, choose the "Console App (.NET Core)" template.

6. Set Up Version Control: It's good practice to use version control for your projects. Visual Studio integrates seamlessly with version control systems like Git. If you're using Git, create a Git repository for your project. You can do this through the "Team Explorer" window in Visual Studio.

7. Explore the Interface: Familiarize yourself with the Visual Studio interface. The IDE consists of various windows, panels, and toolbars that provide access to different features. Spend time exploring the Solution Explorer, Code Editor, Output window, and other panels relevant to your project.

8. Install Extensions: Visual Studio supports extensions that enhance its functionality. Visit the Visual Studio Marketplace to discover and install extensions tailored to your needs. For example, you can install extensions for additional language support, code analysis, or integration with cloud services.

9. Update SDKs and Libraries: Regularly update the software development kits (SDKs) and libraries associated with your project. Updates often include bug fixes, new features, and performance improvements. Visual Studio provides tools to manage SDKs and libraries for your projects.

10. Start Coding: With your development environment set up, you're ready to start coding. Create new code files, write code, and experiment with the features offered by Visual Studio. Take advantage of code completion, debugging tools, and other productivity features as you write your code.

Setting up your development environment in Microsoft Visual Studio is an essential foundation for your coding journey. By following these steps and customizing your environment to suit your preferences, you'll be well-prepared to create, debug, and deploy high-quality software applications using the powerful tools that Visual Studio provides.

CHAPTER II
Getting Started with Visual Studio

2.1 Navigating the Visual Studio Interface

Navigating the Visual Studio interface is an essential skill that every developer should master. The interface is designed to provide you with easy access to various tools, windows, and features that aid in your coding journey. In this section, we will take a detailed look at the different components of the Visual Studio interface and guide you on how to navigate through them effectively.

Understanding the Visual Studio Interface:

1. Menu Bar: The menu bar at the top of the Visual Studio window contains various menus such as File, Edit, View, Project, Debug, and more. These menus house commands and options that allow you to perform different tasks within the IDE.

2. Toolbar: The toolbar is located just below the menu bar and provides quick access to frequently used commands. You can find buttons for actions like building, debugging, running code, and more.

3. Solution Explorer: The Solution Explorer is your hub for managing projects and files. It displays the hierarchy of your project, including folders, files, and resources. You can use it to add, remove, and organize files, as well as manage references.

4. Code Editor: The Code Editor is where you write, edit, and view your code. It offers features like syntax highlighting, code completion, and IntelliSense suggestions. You can open multiple code files in tabs within the Code Editor.

5. Toolbox: The Toolbox provides a collection of controls and components that you can drag and drop into your code to build user interfaces. It's particularly useful for designing forms, user interfaces, and visual elements.

6. Properties Window: This window displays properties and settings for the currently selected element, such as controls, forms, or project settings. You can modify properties directly from this window.

7. Error List: The Error List displays compilation and runtime errors, warnings, and messages related to your code. Clicking on an error takes you to the corresponding line in the Code Editor.

8. Output Window: The Output Window shows the output of various actions, such as build progress, debug information, and console output. It's a useful tool for diagnosing issues and monitoring program behavior.

9. Solution Platforms and Configuration: Visual Studio allows you to build your project for different platforms (e.g., x86, x64) and configurations (e.g., Debug, Release). You can manage these settings through the Solution Platforms dropdown and Configuration Manager.

Navigating Through the Interface:

1. Opening Projects: To open an existing project, go to the File menu and select "Open" or "Open Project/Solution." Browse to the location of your project's solution file (.sln) and select it. The Solution Explorer will display your project's hierarchy.

2. Creating New Files: Right-click on a project or folder in the Solution Explorer and select "Add" to create new files. Choose the appropriate item, such as a class, interface, or form. You can also use the New Item dialog from the Project menu.

3. Tabs and Windows: Visual Studio allows you to open multiple code files simultaneously in separate tabs. You can also drag tabs to create floating windows for better multitasking.

4. Navigating Code: Use keyboard shortcuts like Ctrl + F for searching, Ctrl + G for jumping to a specific line, and Ctrl + B for setting or navigating to breakpoints.

5. Building and Running: Use the Build menu or the Build button on the toolbar to compile your code. Press F5 to start debugging and run your application. You can also use Ctrl + F5 to run without debugging.

6. Viewing Output: If you encounter errors, check the Error List and Output Window for details. Click on an error to navigate directly to the problematic code.

7. Changing Layout: Customize the layout of windows and toolbars based on your preferences. Use the Window menu to access predefined layouts or create your own.

Mastering the art of navigating the Visual Studio interface is pivotal to becoming an efficient and productive developer. By understanding the various components and learning how to use them effectively, you'll be able to seamlessly create, edit, and manage your code, leading to successful software development projects.

2.2. Creating a New Project

Creating a new project in Microsoft Visual Studio is the first step toward building your software application. Whether you're developing a desktop, web, or mobile application, Visual Studio provides a streamlined process for setting up your project. In this section, we will guide you through the process of creating a new project using Visual Studio.

Step-by-Step Guide to Creating a New Project:

1. Open Visual Studio: Launch Microsoft Visual Studio on your computer. You can find it in your Start menu or taskbar if you have it installed.

2. Start a New Project: Once Visual Studio is open, you'll be presented with the Start Page. Click on the "Create a new project" link to begin.

3. Choose a Project Template: In the New Project dialog, you'll see a list of project templates organized by programming language and project type. For example, you can choose from templates for C#, VB.NET, ASP.NET, and more. Select the template that best matches your application's requirements.

4. Configure Project Settings: After selecting a template, you'll need to configure the project settings. This may include specifying the project name, location, solution name, and other relevant options. Some project templates also allow you to choose a target platform, such as Windows, Web, or Mobile.

5. Choose a Framework: Depending on your project type, you may need to select a framework. For example, if you're creating a web application, you might choose between ASP.NET Core or ASP.NET Framework. Choose the appropriate framework version based on your needs.

6. Configure Additional Options: Some project templates may have additional configuration options, such as authentication settings, database connection strings, and more. Configure these options as needed for your application.

7. Create the Project: Once you've configured all the settings, click the "Create" button. Visual Studio will generate the project files and set up the project structure based on your selections.

8. Exploring the Solution Explorer: After creating the project, the Solution Explorer window will appear. This window displays the files and folders in your project's hierarchy. You can add, remove, and organize files using this window.

9. Writing Code: Double-click on a code file in the Solution Explorer to open it in the Code Editor. Here, you can start writing your application's logic using the chosen programming language.

10. Building and Running: Use the Build menu or toolbar button to compile your code. If your project is a console application, you can run it directly from the IDE. For web or other applications, you may need to set a startup project and run it using the appropriate runtime.

11. Adding Functionality: Depending on your project type, you can start adding functionality to your application. For example, if you're building a web application, you can create controllers, views, and models. If it's a desktop application, you can design forms and add event handlers.

12. Testing and Debugging: Visual Studio provides powerful debugging tools to help you identify and fix issues in your code. Use breakpoints, watch windows, and the Immediate window to inspect variables and step through code execution.

13. Saving Your Work: Remember to save your project frequently to avoid losing your progress. Use the Save All command (Ctrl + Shift + S) to save all open files and the project.

By following these steps, you can easily create a new project in Microsoft Visual Studio and start building your application. The process may vary slightly depending on the project template and type you choose, but the general workflow remains consistent. With a new project set up, you're ready to begin coding and bringing your software ideas to life.

2.3. Writing Your First Code

Now that you've created a new project in Microsoft Visual Studio, it's time to start writing your first lines of code. In this section, we will guide you through the process of writing a simple "Hello, World!" program using Visual Studio.

Step-by-Step Guide to Writing Your First Code:

1. Open Your Project: Launch Microsoft Visual Studio and open the project you created in the previous section.

2. Locate the Code File: In the Solution Explorer window, locate the code file where you want to write your first code. For example, if you're working with a C# console application, you might look for a file named `Program.cs`.

3. Open the Code File: Double-click on the code file to open it in the Code Editor. This is where you'll write your code.

4. Write Your Code: In the Code Editor, start by typing the following code:

```csharp
using System;

namespace HelloWorldApp
{
    class Program
    {
        static void Main(string[] args)
        {
```

```
        Console.WriteLine("Hello, World!");

    }

  }

}
```

This is a simple C# console application that prints "Hello, World!" to the console.

5. Understanding the Code: Let's break down the code you just wrote:

 - `using System;`: This line includes the `System` namespace, which provides fundamental types and classes.

 - `namespace HelloWorldApp`: This defines a namespace named `HelloWorldApp` to organize your code.

 - `class Program`: This declares a class named `Program`, which contains your program's logic.

 - `static void Main(string[] args)`: This is the entry point of your program. Code execution starts here.

 - `Console.WriteLine("Hello, World!");`: This line uses the `Console` class to write text to the console.

6. Save Your Code: After writing the code, save the file by clicking the "Save" button in the toolbar or using the Ctrl + S shortcut.

7. Build and Run: To see your program in action, build and run it. Click the "Start" button or use the F5 shortcut. The console window should appear, displaying the "Hello, World!" message.

8. Exploring Output: After running the program, you'll see the output in the console window. You can experiment by modifying the code and observing how it affects the output.

9. Debugging: If you encounter any issues or errors, Visual Studio provides debugging tools to help you identify and fix problems. Set breakpoints, step through code, and inspect variables to understand the program's behavior.

10. Experiment and Learn: Now that you've written and executed your first code, feel free to experiment with different statements, variables, and logic. Try creating simple calculations, user interactions, or other programming concepts.

By following these steps, you've successfully written and executed your first code using Microsoft Visual Studio. This simple "Hello, World!" example demonstrates the basic process of coding, saving, building, and running a program. As you continue your coding journey, you'll explore more complex projects and learn about advanced coding techniques and practices.

CHAPTER III
Exploring Programming Languages in Visual Studio

3.1 Introduction to Different Programming Languages

In the world of software development, there is a wide variety of programming languages, each with its own syntax, features, and use cases. As a developer using Microsoft Visual Studio, it's important to have a basic understanding of some of the prominent programming languages that you can work with. This chapter introduces you to different programming languages supported by Visual Studio and provides insights into their characteristics and typical applications.

Overview of Programming Languages:

1. C#: C# (pronounced "C sharp") is a versatile and widely used programming language developed by Microsoft. It is especially popular for building Windows applications, web applications, and games using the Unity game engine. C# is known for its strong type system, rich standard library, and support for object-oriented programming.

2. Visual Basic .NET (VB.NET): VB.NET is another language developed by Microsoft and is part of the .NET framework. It is designed to be easy to learn and use, making it a great choice for beginners. VB.NET is commonly used for developing Windows applications and web services.

3. JavaScript: JavaScript is a scripting language commonly used for building interactive web applications. It runs in web browsers and allows developers to add dynamic behavior to web pages. Visual Studio provides tools for developing and debugging JavaScript code, making it easier to create engaging web experiences.

4. Python: Python is a versatile and easy-to-read programming language that emphasizes code readability. It is widely used for web development, data analysis, artificial intelligence, and scientific computing. Visual Studio supports Python development with features like IntelliSense and debugging.

5. C++: C++ is an extension of the C programming language and is often used for system programming, game development, and performance-critical applications. It provides low-level memory manipulation and supports both procedural and object-oriented programming paradigms.

6. F#: F# is a functional-first programming language in the .NET ecosystem. It focuses on functional programming concepts and is suitable for data-centric and analytical applications. F# is often used for financial modeling, scientific computing, and data processing.

Exploring Different Languages in Visual Studio:

1. Creating Projects: Visual Studio provides templates for creating projects in different programming languages. You can select the appropriate template based on your chosen language and application type. For example, you can create a C# Windows Forms application or a Python web application.

2. Syntax Highlighting: As you write code in Visual Studio, the editor provides syntax highlighting specific to the programming language you're using. This makes it easier to identify keywords, variables, and other elements in your code.

3. IntelliSense: Visual Studio offers IntelliSense, a feature that provides context-aware suggestions and autocompletions as you type code. This is especially helpful for avoiding syntax errors and increasing your coding speed.

4. Debugging: Regardless of the programming language you're working with, Visual Studio offers powerful debugging capabilities. You can set breakpoints, inspect variables, and step through code to identify and fix issues in your programs.

Choosing the Right Language for Your Project:

When deciding which programming language to use for a specific project, consider the following factors:

- Project requirements and goals

- Existing codebase and technology stack

- Team expertise and familiarity with the language

- Performance and scalability requirements

- Community support and available libraries

By familiarizing yourself with different programming languages and understanding their strengths and use cases, you'll be better equipped to choose the most suitable language for your projects and make the most out of Microsoft Visual Studio's capabilities.

3.2. Writing Code in C#

C# (pronounced "C sharp") is a powerful and versatile programming language developed by Microsoft. It is widely used for building a variety of applications, including Windows desktop applications, web applications, cloud services, and games. In this section, we'll delve into the process of writing code in C# using Microsoft Visual Studio.

Setting Up Your Environment:

Before you start writing C# code, ensure that you have Microsoft Visual Studio installed on your machine. If not, you can download and install it from the official Microsoft Visual Studio website. Once you have Visual Studio installed, follow these steps to create a new C# project:

1. Launch Microsoft Visual Studio.

2. Click on "File" in the top menu, then select "New" > "Project."

3. In the "New Project" dialog box, select "Console App (.NET Core)" under the "Create a new project" section.

4. Choose a name and location for your project, then click "Create."

Writing Your First C# Program:

Once you've created a new C# project in Visual Studio, you're ready to write your first C# program. Follow these steps to create a simple "Hello, World!" program:

1. In the Solution Explorer panel on the right, find the "Program.cs" file under the "Program" folder.

2. Double-click on "Program.cs" to open it in the code editor.

You'll see the default C# code that Visual Studio generates for a new console application:

```csharp
using System;

namespace YourNamespace
{
```

```
  class Program
  {
      static void Main(string[] args)
      {
          Console.WriteLine("Hello, World!");
      }
  }
}
```

Understanding the Code:

- The `using System;` statement is used to include the `System` namespace, which provides fundamental classes and base classes.

- The `namespace` declaration encloses a collection of related classes and methods. Replace `YourNamespace` with the desired namespace for your project.

- Inside the namespace, the `Program` class is defined. This class contains the `Main` method, which serves as the entry point for your application.

- The `Main` method is where the execution of your program begins. In this example, it simply prints "Hello, World!" to the console.

Running Your Program:

To run your C# program, follow these steps:

1. Save any changes you've made to the code.

2. Press the green "Start" button ( ) located in the top menu of Visual Studio.

3. The output of your program will appear in the "Output" panel at the bottom of the Visual Studio window.

Congratulations! You've successfully written and executed your first C# program using Microsoft Visual Studio.

Further Exploration:

Now that you've created a basic "Hello, World!" program in C#, you can explore more advanced concepts such as variables, data types, conditional statements, loops, and functions. Visual Studio provides a wealth of resources and tools for learning and practicing C# programming. You can also explore the extensive documentation and tutorials available on the official Microsoft C# documentation website.

As you continue your journey in learning C# and programming with Visual Studio, you'll be well-equipped to create a wide range of applications and take advantage of the features and capabilities of this versatile programming language.

3.3. Writing Code in Python

Python is a versatile and widely-used programming language known for its simplicity and readability. It is commonly used for web development, data analysis, scientific computing, artificial intelligence, and more. Microsoft Visual Studio provides robust support for Python development, making it a popular choice for Python programmers. In this section, we will explore how to write and run Python code in Visual Studio.

Setting Up Your Environment:

Before you begin writing Python code in Visual Studio, ensure that you have the Python extension installed. If not, you can install it from the Visual Studio Marketplace. Follow these steps to create a new Python project:

1. Launch Microsoft Visual Studio.

2. Click on "File" in the top menu, then select "New" > "Project."

3. In the "New Project" dialog box, select "Python" under the "Create a new project" section.

4. Choose a name and location for your project, then click "Create."

Writing Your First Python Program:

Once you've created a new Python project in Visual Studio, you're ready to write your first Python program. Follow these steps to create a simple "Hello, World!" program:

1. In the Solution Explorer panel on the right, find the "Program.py" file.

2. Double-click on "Program.py" to open it in the code editor.

You'll see an empty Python file. Type the following code to print "Hello, World!" to the console:

```python
print("Hello, World!")
```

Running Your Program:

To run your Python program, follow these steps:

1. Save any changes you've made to the code.

2. Press the green "Start" button (▶) located in the top menu of Visual Studio.

3. The output of your program will appear in the "Output" panel at the bottom of the Visual Studio window.

Exploring Python Development in Visual Studio:

Visual Studio offers a rich set of features to enhance your Python development experience:

- **IntelliSense:** Visual Studio provides intelligent code completion, suggestions, and auto-completion for Python code.

- **Debugging:** You can set breakpoints, step through code, and inspect variables using Visual Studio's powerful debugging tools.

- **Integrated Terminal:** Visual Studio includes an integrated terminal that allows you to run Python scripts and commands directly within the IDE.

- **Package Management:** You can manage Python packages and dependencies using the built-in package manager.

Further Learning:

As you become more comfortable with writing Python code in Visual Studio, you can explore more advanced topics, such as working with libraries, data manipulation, web development frameworks, and more. Microsoft provides extensive documentation and tutorials for Python development in Visual Studio, which can help you deepen your understanding and expand your skills.

By leveraging the capabilities of Visual Studio, you'll be well-equipped to write, test, and debug Python applications efficiently and effectively, whether you're a beginner or an experienced Python developer.

3.4. Choosing the Right Language for Your Project

When embarking on a coding project, one of the critical decisions you'll need to make is choosing the right programming language. Different programming languages offer distinct features, libraries, and ecosystems that cater to specific types of projects. In this section, we'll discuss the factors to consider when selecting a programming language for your project and how Visual Studio can assist you in this decision-making process.

Factors to Consider:

1. Project Requirements: Consider the specific requirements of your project. Is it a web application, a mobile app, a desktop software, data analysis, or machine learning? Different languages are better suited for different types of projects.

2. Language Familiarity: Your familiarity with a programming language plays a significant role in the decision. If you're proficient in a particular language, it may be more efficient to stick with it.

3. Community and Support: A robust community and active support forums can be invaluable when you encounter challenges during development. Consider languages with large and active communities.

4. Performance: Some languages are optimized for performance, making them suitable for resource-intensive tasks, while others are more geared towards rapid development.

5. Integration and Ecosystem: Consider the availability of libraries, frameworks, and tools that can streamline your development process. Certain languages have well-established ecosystems for specific domains.

Using Visual Studio to Choose a Language:

Visual Studio offers tools and features that can help you make an informed decision about the programming language for your project:

1. Language Support: Visual Studio supports a wide range of programming languages, from C# and C++ to Python, JavaScript, and more. You can install language-specific extensions to enhance your coding experience.

2. Code Samples and Templates: Visual Studio provides a variety of code samples and templates for different languages and project types. These templates can give you a head start in your project and showcase the capabilities of each language.

3. IntelliCode: Visual Studio's IntelliCode suggests code completions based on commonly used patterns and practices. This feature can give you insights into how different languages handle similar tasks.

4. Performance Profiling: If performance is a critical factor, Visual Studio's performance profiling tools can help you analyze how different languages perform in specific scenarios.

Example Scenario:

Let's say you're considering building a web application. You have experience with both Python and JavaScript. Here's how Visual Studio can assist you in making a decision:

1. Language Features: Explore the features of Python and JavaScript. Python's simplicity and readability may make it suitable for backend development, while JavaScript's dominance in web development may make it a strong candidate for frontend work.

2. Templates: Create a new web application project using both Python and JavaScript templates in Visual Studio. This will allow you to examine the structure and components of each project type.

3. IntelliCode: As you start writing code, observe how Visual Studio's IntelliCode assists you in each language. Are you getting relevant code suggestions and completions for both?

4. Performance Testing: If performance is a concern, use Visual Studio's performance profiling tools to compare the execution speed of critical functions in both languages.

Conclusion:

Choosing the right programming language is a crucial step in ensuring the success of your coding project. By leveraging the features and tools provided by Visual Studio, you can make an informed decision based on your project's requirements, your familiarity with the language, community support, and performance considerations. Ultimately, Visual Studio empowers you to explore different languages and make an educated choice that aligns with your project goals.

CHAPTER IV
Essential Tools and Features in Visual Studio

4.1 Using the Code Editor and IntelliSense

The code editor is the heart of your development environment in Visual Studio. It's where you write, edit, and manage your code files. Combined with IntelliSense, a powerful code completion and suggestion feature, the code editor in Visual Studio significantly enhances your coding experience. In this section, we'll delve into how to efficiently utilize the code editor and make the most out of IntelliSense.

Understanding the Code Editor:

The code editor in Visual Studio provides a clean and organized interface for writing code. It offers various features that help you write and manage code more effectively:

1. Syntax Highlighting: Visual Studio highlights different elements of your code with distinct colors, making it easier to identify keywords, variables, and other code components.

2. Auto-Indentation: The code editor automatically indents your code as you write, ensuring consistent and readable formatting.

3. Code Folding: You can collapse sections of code to focus on specific parts of your codebase, improving readability.

4. Navigation: Use keyboard shortcuts or the navigation bar to quickly move between different parts of your code.

Harnessing the Power of IntelliSense:

IntelliSense is a feature in Visual Studio that offers code completion, suggestions, and context-aware assistance as you type. Here's how to make the most of IntelliSense:

1. Code Completion: As you type, IntelliSense suggests code completions based on the context. Pressing Tab or Enter will insert the selected suggestion. For example, if you're typing a method call, IntelliSense will display available methods and their parameters.

2. Parameter Info: When calling a function or method, IntelliSense displays information about the required parameters and their types, helping you avoid errors.

3. Quick Info: Hover over a code element to see a tooltip with additional information, such as the type of a variable or a brief description of a method.

4. Smart Suggestions: IntelliSense learns from your coding patterns and suggests appropriate code snippets, making repetitive tasks quicker.

Example: Using IntelliSense in C# Programming:

Let's say you're writing C# code for a simple console application that calculates the area of a circle. Here's how you can leverage the code editor and IntelliSense:

1. Start Typing: Begin typing the code to calculate the area of a circle using the formula `area = π * radius * radius`.

2. Auto-Completion: As you type `Math.` after `π *`, IntelliSense displays a list of available math functions. Select `PI` from the list, and it will auto-complete the constant value of π.

3. Parameter Info: When you type `Math.Pow(` for calculating the square of the radius, IntelliSense will show parameter information. Enter the `radius` variable and `, 2)` to raise it to the power of 2.

4. Quick Info: Hover over the `Math.PI` constant or the `Math.Pow` method to see tooltips with additional details.

Customizing IntelliSense:

You can customize IntelliSense to suit your preferences. Go to `Tools > Options > Text Editor > [Language] > IntelliSense` to adjust settings like the delay before suggestions appear and the type of suggestions you want to see.

Conclusion:

The code editor and IntelliSense are essential tools in Visual Studio that greatly streamline your coding process. By understanding and utilizing their features effectively, you can write code more efficiently, reduce errors, and enhance your overall development experience. Experiment with different settings and practice using IntelliSense to become a more proficient coder in Visual Studio.

4.2. Debugging Your Code

Debugging is an indispensable skill for developers. It's the process of identifying and fixing errors, or bugs, in your code. Visual Studio provides a robust set of debugging tools and features that help you track down and resolve issues efficiently. In this section, we'll explore how to effectively debug your code using Visual Studio's debugging capabilities.

Getting Started with Debugging:

1. Setting Breakpoints: A breakpoint is a designated spot in your code where the debugger will pause execution. To set a breakpoint, simply click in the gutter area next to the line number in the code editor. When your program hits a breakpoint, it will pause, allowing you to inspect variables and step through the code.

2. Running in Debug Mode: To start debugging, press `F5` or select `Debug > Start Debugging` from the menu. Your program will launch in debug mode, and execution will pause at the first breakpoint encountered.

Exploring the Debugging Toolbar:

Visual Studio's debugging toolbar offers a range of tools to help you navigate through your code while debugging:

1. Step Into (`F11`): Use this option to step into a method call, moving from the current line of code to the first line of the method being called.

2. Step Over (`F10`): This option allows you to move to the next line of code, skipping over method calls. If the next line is a method call, it will be executed, but you won't delve into its implementation.

3. Step Out (`Shift + F11`): If you're inside a method and want to quickly exit and continue debugging at the calling line, use this option.

4. Continue (`F5`): Resume program execution until the next breakpoint is encountered or until the program completes.

Inspecting Variables:

While debugging, you can examine the values of variables and expressions to understand what's happening at different points in your code:

1. Locals Window: This window displays variables and their values within the current scope. To open it, go to `Debug > Windows > Locals` or use the shortcut `Ctrl + Alt + V, L`.

2. Watch Window: The watch window allows you to add specific variables or expressions to track. Right-click and select `Add Watch` to monitor values. Open it via `Debug > Windows > Watch` or `Ctrl + Alt + W, W`.

3. Immediate Window: Use this window to execute expressions or commands while debugging. It's a great place for quick tests. Open it via `Debug > Windows > Immediate` or `Ctrl + Alt + I`.

Breakpoint Options:

1. Conditional Breakpoints: Right-click a breakpoint and set a condition. Execution will only pause if the condition evaluates to true.

2. Hit Count: You can specify how many times a breakpoint must be hit before the debugger activates.

Example: Debugging in Action:

Let's consider a scenario where you're building a C# application that calculates the factorial of a number. However, there's a logical error causing incorrect results. Here's how you can debug it:

1. Setting Breakpoints: Place a breakpoint at the line where the factorial calculation occurs.

2. Running in Debug Mode: Start debugging, and the program will pause at the breakpoint. Use the debugging toolbar to step through the code, monitoring variable values in the Locals Window.

3. Inspecting Variables: Add the `factorial` variable to the Watch Window to track its value as you step through the code.

4. Identifying the Bug: As you step through, you notice that the `factorial` variable is being multiplied by 0. With this insight, you can correct the bug and rerun the program.

Conclusion:

Debugging is a fundamental skill that every developer should master. Visual Studio's debugging features empower you to diagnose and resolve issues efficiently, ensuring your code functions as intended. By utilizing breakpoints, debugging toolbar options, and variable inspection tools, you can effectively identify and fix bugs in your code. Practice debugging different scenarios to sharpen your debugging skills and streamline your development process.

4.3. Version Control with Git Integration

Version control is a crucial aspect of modern software development, enabling collaboration, tracking changes, and facilitating code management. Git, a distributed version control system, has become the de facto standard in the development community. Microsoft Visual Studio provides seamless integration with Git, allowing you to manage your codebase efficiently. In this section, we'll explore how to use Git within Visual Studio for version control.

Setting Up Git Integration:

1. Install Git: If you don't have Git installed, download and install it from the official website (https://git-scm.com/).

2. Configure Git: Set your name and email in Git configuration using these commands in the command-line interface:

```
git config --global user.name "Your Name"
git config --global user.email "your@email.com"
```

3. Connecting to a Repository: To start using Git in Visual Studio, open the Team Explorer window (`Ctrl + \, Ctrl + M`) and click on "Manage Connections" to connect to a Git repository.

Creating and Cloning Repositories:

1. Creating a Repository: To create a new Git repository for your project, go to `File > Add to Source Control` and choose Git.

2. Cloning a Repository: To clone an existing repository, go to `File > Clone Repository` and provide the repository's URL.

Using Git in Visual Studio:

1. Viewing Changes: The "Changes" window in Team Explorer displays all the changes made to your files. You can review each change, stage them, and write a commit message.

2. Staging Changes: Select the changes you want to include in the next commit and click "Stage" to add them to the staging area.

3. Committing Changes: After staging changes, provide a meaningful commit message and click "Commit" to save your changes.

4. Viewing History: Use the "History" window to see the commit history of your project. You can compare different versions and view the changes made in each commit.

Branching and Merging:

1. Creating Branches: In Team Explorer, click "New Branch" to create a new branch for your work. Give it a descriptive name and choose the base branch.

2. Switching Branches: Use the "Branches" dropdown in Team Explorer to switch between branches.

3. Merging Changes: To merge changes from one branch into another, right-click on the target branch and choose "Merge from..." to select the source branch.

Resolving Merge Conflicts:

1. Conflicts: When merging or pulling changes, conflicts may arise if the same lines of code were modified in different branches. Visual Studio provides a conflict resolution tool to help you resolve these conflicts.

2. Resolving Conflicts: Open the file with conflicts, and Visual Studio will show you the conflicting sections. Manually edit the file to resolve conflicts, then stage and commit the changes.

Pushing and Pulling Changes:

1. Pushing Changes: Use the "Push" button in Team Explorer to send your committed changes to the remote repository.

2. Pulling Changes: To update your local repository with changes from the remote repository, use the "Pull" button.

Example: Using Git in Visual Studio:

Imagine you're working on a web application and want to implement a new feature. Here's how you would use Git in Visual Studio:

1. Creating a Branch: Start by creating a new branch for your feature. Give it a meaningful name related to the feature.

2. Coding and Committing: Write the code for your feature and make commits as you progress.

3. Pushing Changes: Push your changes to the remote repository regularly to keep your branch up to date.

4. Resolving Conflicts: If another team member makes changes to the same files, conflicts may occur when you try to merge. Resolve conflicts by editing the conflicting sections in Visual Studio.

5. Merging and Testing: Once your feature is complete, merge your branch into the main development branch. Test thoroughly to ensure everything works as expected.

Conclusion:

Git integration within Visual Studio streamlines version control for your projects. By understanding how to create repositories, commit changes, manage branches, and resolve conflicts, you can effectively collaborate with team members and maintain a well-organized codebase. Visual Studio's Git integration empowers you to work confidently and efficiently on your software projects while benefiting from the power of version control.

4.4. Customizing Your Development Environment

Customizing your development environment in Microsoft Visual Studio can greatly enhance your productivity and streamline your workflow. Visual Studio provides a range of customization options that allow you to tailor the IDE (Integrated Development Environment) to your preferences. In this section, we'll explore various ways to personalize your development environment.

1. Themes and Color Schemes:

Visual Studio offers a variety of themes and color schemes to change the look and feel of the IDE. To customize your theme:

- Go to `Tools > Options > Environment > General`.

- Choose your preferred theme from the "Color theme" dropdown.

You can also install additional themes from the Visual Studio Marketplace.

2. Keyboard Shortcuts:

Customizing keyboard shortcuts can significantly speed up your coding process. To modify or add keyboard shortcuts:

- Go to `Tools > Options > Environment > Keyboard`.

- Search for commands and assign new shortcuts according to your preference.

3. Tool Windows:

You can arrange, dock, and hide tool windows based on your workflow:

- To dock a tool window, drag it to the desired location in the IDE.

- To hide a tool window, click the close button on its tab.

4. Window Layouts:

Save and switch between different window layouts to suit various tasks:

- Create and save custom layouts via `Window > Save Window Layout`.

- Switch between layouts using `Window > Apply Window Layout`.

5. Extensions and Add-ons:

Visual Studio supports a wide range of extensions that add functionality to the IDE. To install extensions:

- Go to `Extensions > Manage Extensions`.
- Browse or search for desired extensions and click "Install".

6. Code Snippets:

Code snippets are predefined code templates that you can insert using shortcuts. Create custom code snippets or use built-in ones:

- Open the `Code Snippets Manager` from `Tools > Code Snippets Manager`.
- Choose a language and import or create new snippets.

7. IntelliCode:

IntelliCode suggests contextually relevant code completions based on your coding patterns:

- Install the "IntelliCode" extension from the Visual Studio Marketplace.
- Configure IntelliCode settings under `Tools > Options > IntelliCode`.

8. Git Integration:

Customize how Visual Studio works with Git:

- Configure Git settings via `Team Explorer > Settings > Repository Settings`.

9. Window Tabs:

Customize the behavior of window tabs:

- Go to `Tools > Options > Environment > Tabs and Windows`.
- Adjust tab behavior, such as open document tabs in a single row.

10. Debugging Layouts:

Customize the layout of debugging windows:

- Create custom debugging layouts via the `Debug > Windows Layouts` menu.

Example: Customizing Themes

Let's say you prefer a dark-themed environment for coding. To customize the theme:

1. Go to `Tools > Options > Environment > General`.

2. Choose "Dark" from the "Color theme" dropdown.

3. Click "OK" to apply the new theme.

Conclusion:

Customizing your development environment in Visual Studio empowers you to create a workspace that aligns with your preferences and workflow. By adjusting themes, keyboard shortcuts, tool windows, and other settings, you can optimize your efficiency and comfort while working on projects. Visual Studio's flexibility ensures that you can create a personalized coding environment that enhances your coding experience.

CHAPTER V
Building Basic Applications

5.1 Creating a Console Application

A console application is a simple type of application that interacts with the user through a command-line interface. It's a great way to learn the basics of programming and get familiar with the development process in Microsoft Visual Studio. In this section, we'll walk you through the steps of creating a console application using Visual Studio.

Step 1: Opening Visual Studio and Creating a New Project

1. Launch Microsoft Visual Studio.

2. Go to `File > New > Project`.

3. In the "Create a new project" dialog, select "Console App (.NET Core)" under the "Create a new project" section.

4. Choose a location to save your project and provide a name for it. Click the "Create" button.

Step 2: Writing Code

Once the project is created, you'll see the default code for a simple "Hello World" application.

```csharp
```

```
using System;

namespace MyConsoleApp
{
    class Program
    {
        static void Main(string[] args)
        {
            Console.WriteLine("Hello, World!");
        }
    }
}
```

The `Main` method is the entry point of your application. The `Console.WriteLine` statement prints the text "Hello, World!" to the console.

Step 3: Running the Application

1. To run your application, simply press the `F5` key or click the "Start" button on the toolbar.

    ![Run Application](https://example.com/run_application.png)

2. The console window will open, and you'll see the output of your program:

```
Hello, World!
```

Step 4: Modifying the Code

Let's modify the code to create a simple interactive program that takes user input and displays a personalized message:

```csharp
using System;

namespace MyConsoleApp
{
    class Program
    {
        static void Main(string[] args)
        {
            Console.Write("Enter your name: ");
            string name = Console.ReadLine();

            Console.WriteLine($"Hello, {name}!");
        }
    }
}
```

```
```

In this version of the program, we use `Console.Write` to prompt the user for their name, and `Console.ReadLine` to read their input. We then use string interpolation (`$`) to display a personalized greeting.

Step 5: Running the Modified Application

1. Build and run the modified application using the same steps as before.

2. The program will now prompt you to enter your name. After entering your name and pressing `Enter`, the program will display a personalized greeting:

```
Enter your name: John
Hello, John!
```

Conclusion:

Creating a console application is a fundamental step in learning programming using Microsoft Visual Studio. This simple example demonstrates how to create, write, modify, and run a basic console application. As you become more comfortable with the development environment, you can explore more complex applications and gradually learn advanced programming concepts.

5.2. Building a Simple GUI Application

Graphical User Interface (GUI) applications provide a more user-friendly way to interact with software compared to command-line interfaces. In this section, we'll explore how to create a basic GUI application using Microsoft Visual Studio.

Step 1: Creating a New Windows Forms Project

1. Open Microsoft Visual Studio.

2. Go to `File > New > Project`.

3. In the "Create a new project" dialog, select "Windows Forms App (.NET Core)" under the "Create a new project" section.

4. Choose a location to save your project and provide a name for it. Click the "Create" button.

Step 2: Designing the GUI

Once the project is created, you'll see the Windows Forms Designer.

1. From the Toolbox on the left, drag and drop controls onto the form. Let's add a `Label`, a `TextBox`, and a `Button`.

2. Select the controls you added and set their properties in the Properties window on the right. For example, you can set the text of the label and the button.

Step 3: Writing Code for the GUI

1. Double-click the button to generate an event handler for its click event. This will take you to the code-behind file.

2. Write code to handle the button click event. For instance, let's create a simple program that takes a user's name from the text box and displays a personalized greeting in a message box:

```csharp
using System;
using System.Windows.Forms;

namespace MySimpleGuiApp
{
    public partial class MainForm : Form
    {
        public MainForm()
        {
            InitializeComponent();
        }

        private void buttonGreet_Click(object sender, EventArgs e)
        {
            string name = textBoxName.Text;
            MessageBox.Show($"Hello, {name}!", "Greeting");
        }
    }
```

```
}
```
```
```

In this example, we use the `buttonGreet_Click` event handler to get the text from the `textBoxName` control and display a message box with a personalized greeting.

Step 4: Running the GUI Application

1. Build and run the application using the same steps as before.

2. The GUI application will open, displaying the controls you added. Enter your name in the text box and click the "Greet" button.

3. A message box will appear with the personalized greeting:

Conclusion:

Creating a simple GUI application using Windows Forms in Microsoft Visual Studio allows you to create interactive programs that provide a more engaging user experience. This example demonstrates how to design a basic GUI, write code to handle events, and create a simple interaction with the user. As you become more comfortable with GUI development, you can explore more advanced features and create more sophisticated applications.

5.3. Working with User Input and Output

User input and output are fundamental aspects of any application. In this section, we will explore how to handle user input and provide meaningful output in a GUI application using Microsoft Visual Studio.

Step 1: Adding Controls for User Input and Output

1. Open the Windows Forms project you created in the previous sections.

2. In the Windows Forms Designer, add the following controls to your form:

- Label: This will provide instructions to the user.

- TextBox: This is where the user can enter input.

- Button: This will trigger an action based on the input.

- Label or TextBox: This is where the application will display the output.

3. Arrange the controls on the form as needed.

Step 2: Handling User Input

1. Double-click the button control to generate an event handler for its click event. This will take you to the code-behind file.

2. Write code to handle the button click event. Let's create an example where the user enters their age in the text box, and upon clicking the button, the application displays a message indicating whether they are eligible to vote:

```csharp
using System;
using System.Windows.Forms;
```

```csharp
namespace UserInputOutputApp
{
    public partial class MainForm : Form
    {
        public MainForm()
        {
            InitializeComponent();
        }

        private void buttonCheckVote_Click(object sender, EventArgs e)
        {
            int age = Convert.ToInt32(textBoxAge.Text);

            if (age >= 18)
            {
                labelResult.Text = "You are eligible to vote!";
            }
            else
            {
                labelResult.Text = "You are not eligible to vote yet.";
            }
        }
    }
}
```
```
```

In this example, we use the `buttonCheckVote_Click` event handler to retrieve the user's age from the `textBoxAge` control. Based on the age, the application updates the `labelResult` control to display an appropriate message.

Step 3: Running the Application

1. Build and run the application using the same steps as before.

2. Enter an age in the text box and click the "Check Vote Eligibility" button.

3. The application will update the output label with the eligibility status based on the entered age:

Step 4: Handling Different Types of User Input

You can extend this concept to handle various types of user input, such as text, numbers, dates, and more. Utilize appropriate controls and validation techniques to ensure accurate data entry.

Conclusion:

Working with user input and output is crucial for creating interactive and user-friendly applications. This section demonstrated how to capture user input, process it, and provide meaningful output in a GUI application. By understanding event handling and using appropriate controls, you can create applications that efficiently interact with users and provide valuable information or services. As you become more adept, you can explore advanced techniques, such as data validation and error handling, to enhance the user experience even further.

CHAPTER VI
Introduction to Data Structures and Algorithms

6.1 Understanding Data Structures

Data structures are fundamental concepts in computer science that allow us to organize and store data efficiently. They play a crucial role in solving complex problems and optimizing algorithms. In this section, we will delve into the basics of data structures, their types, and their significance in programming using Microsoft Visual Studio.

What are Data Structures?

At its core, a data structure is a way of organizing and storing data in a computer's memory. It defines how the data is stored, accessed, and manipulated. Choosing the right data structure for a particular problem can significantly impact the performance and efficiency of an algorithm.

Types of Data Structures:

1. Arrays: Arrays are collections of elements, each identified by an index or key. They provide fast access to elements but may require contiguous memory allocation.

2. Linked Lists: Linked lists consist of nodes, where each node contains data and a reference (or link) to the next node. They allow dynamic memory allocation and efficient insertion and deletion operations.

3. Stacks: Stacks follow the Last-In-First-Out (LIFO) principle. Elements can be pushed onto the stack and popped off the stack, making it useful for managing function calls and undo operations.

4. Queues: Queues follow the First-In-First-Out (FIFO) principle. Elements are enqueued at the rear and dequeued from the front. They are used in scenarios like task scheduling and breadth-first search.

5. Trees: Trees are hierarchical structures with a root node and child nodes. They include binary trees, AVL trees, and B-trees, among others. Trees are used for efficient searching, sorting, and hierarchical organization.

6. Graphs: Graphs consist of nodes connected by edges. They are used to model relationships between entities and are essential in network analysis and route optimization.

7. Hash Tables: Hash tables (or hash maps) use a hash function to map keys to values, allowing constant-time average retrieval. They are used for fast lookups and associative arrays.

Selecting the Right Data Structure:

The choice of data structure depends on the problem you are trying to solve and the operations you need to perform. Here's a simple example to illustrate this:

Example: Implementing a To-Do List

Suppose you want to create a to-do list application. You need to add tasks, mark them as completed, and remove them. For this scenario:

- You can use an array to store the tasks. However, if you frequently add or remove tasks, linked lists may be a better option due to their efficient insertion and deletion.

- If you want to prioritize tasks, you might use a priority queue.

- If tasks have dependencies, you could represent them using a graph.

Conclusion:

Understanding data structures is essential for efficient and effective programming. By selecting the right data structure for a specific problem, you can improve the performance and readability of your code. As you continue your journey in coding with Microsoft Visual Studio, you'll encounter various data structures and learn how to implement them to solve real-world challenges. The next section will explore algorithms that operate on these data structures to further enhance your coding skills.

6.2. Implementing Basic Algorithms

Algorithms are step-by-step procedures for solving problems or performing specific tasks. They are the heart of computer programming, driving the logic and behavior of software applications. In this section, we will explore some fundamental algorithms and learn how to implement them using Microsoft Visual Studio.

Understanding Algorithm Complexity:

Before diving into specific algorithms, it's important to understand algorithm complexity, which refers to how the runtime or memory usage of an algorithm scales with the input size. Complexity is often classified as time complexity (how long an algorithm takes to run) and space complexity (how much memory an algorithm uses).

Sorting Algorithms:

Sorting is a common operation in programming, and various algorithms exist to accomplish this task. Let's take a look at two classic sorting algorithms:

1. Bubble Sort:

Bubble sort is a simple sorting algorithm that repeatedly steps through the list, compares adjacent elements, and swaps them if they are in the wrong order. This process continues until the entire list is sorted.

```csharp
void BubbleSort(int[] arr) {
    int n = arr.Length;
    for (int i = 0; i < n - 1; i++) {
        for (int j = 0; j < n - i - 1; j++) {
            if (arr[j] > arr[j + 1]) {
                int temp = arr[j];
                arr[j] = arr[j + 1];
                arr[j + 1] = temp;
            }
        }
    }
}
```

2. Quick Sort:

Quick sort is a divide-and-conquer algorithm that selects a "pivot" element and partitions the array into two sub-arrays: elements less than the pivot and elements greater than the pivot. It then recursively sorts the sub-arrays.

```csharp
void QuickSort(int[] arr, int low, int high) {
    if (low < high) {
        int pivotIndex = Partition(arr, low, high);
        QuickSort(arr, low, pivotIndex - 1);
        QuickSort(arr, pivotIndex + 1, high);
    }
}

int Partition(int[] arr, int low, int high) {
    int pivot = arr[high];
    int i = low - 1;
    for (int j = low; j < high; j++) {
        if (arr[j] < pivot) {
            i++;
            int temp = arr[i];
            arr[i] = arr[j];
            arr[j] = temp;
        }
    }
}
```

```csharp
        int temp = arr[i + 1];

        arr[i + 1] = arr[high];

        arr[high] = temp;

        return i + 1;

    }
```

Searching Algorithms:

Searching algorithms aim to locate a specific element within a collection. Let's explore a couple of search algorithms:

1. Binary Search:

   Binary search is an efficient algorithm for finding an item from a sorted list. It repeatedly divides the search range in half until the target element is found or the search range is empty.

```csharp
int BinarySearch(int[] arr, int target) {
    int left = 0, right = arr.Length - 1;
    while (left <= right) {
        int mid = left + (right - left) / 2;
        if (arr[mid] == target) {
            return mid;
        }
        if (arr[mid] < target) {
```

```
            left = mid + 1;

        } else {

            right = mid - 1;

        }

    }

    return -1; // Element not found

}
```

2. Linear Search:

Linear search is a simple search algorithm that iterates through each element in a list and compares it with the target element.

```csharp
int LinearSearch(int[] arr, int target) {

    for (int i = 0; i < arr.Length; i++) {

        if (arr[i] == target) {

            return i;

        }

    }

    return -1; // Element not found

}
```

Recursion:

Recursion is a powerful concept where a function calls itself to solve a smaller instance of a problem. It's often used in algorithms involving tree structures and divide-and-conquer strategies.

Example: Calculating Factorial Using Recursion

```csharp
int Factorial(int n) {
    if (n <= 1) {
        return 1;
    }
    return n * Factorial(n - 1);
}
```

Conclusion:

Understanding and implementing basic algorithms is a foundational skill for any programmer. In this chapter, we've covered sorting and searching algorithms, as well as the concept of recursion. These algorithms serve as building blocks for more complex tasks, and by mastering them, you'll be better equipped to tackle a wide range of programming challenges using Microsoft Visual Studio. As you continue your coding journey, you'll have the tools to optimize your code and create efficient and robust software solutions.

6.3. Using Visual Studio for Algorithm Development

In this section, we will explore how to leverage the power of Microsoft Visual Studio for developing and testing algorithms. Visual Studio provides a comprehensive set of tools and features that can greatly aid in algorithm implementation, testing, and optimization. Whether you are a beginner or an experienced programmer, Visual Studio's capabilities can enhance your algorithm development process.

Creating a New Project:

1. Launch Microsoft Visual Studio and select "Create a new project."

2. Choose the appropriate project template based on the programming language you are using (e.g., C# Console Application, Python Application).

3. Name your project and select a location to save it.

4. Click "Create" to generate your project.

Writing and Testing Algorithms:

1. Once your project is created, open the code editor window.

2. Begin writing your algorithm code. You can define your functions, data structures, and logic as needed.

3. Leverage Visual Studio's IntelliSense feature to autocomplete code, suggest method names, and provide parameter details.

4. Use the built-in debugging tools to step through your algorithm's execution and monitor variable values. Set breakpoints to pause execution and examine the state of your code.

5. Utilize the Immediate Window to execute code and evaluate expressions during debugging.

Example: Fibonacci Sequence Algorithm in C#

```csharp
using System;

class Program {
    static int Fibonacci(int n) {
        if (n <= 1) {
            return n;
        }
        return Fibonacci(n - 1) + Fibonacci(n - 2);
    }


    static void Main(string[] args) {
        Console.WriteLine("Enter the number of terms: ");
        int count = Convert.ToInt32(Console.ReadLine());


        for (int i = 0; i < count; i++) {
            Console.Write(Fibonacci(i) + " ");
        }
    }
}
```

Performance Analysis:

Visual Studio provides tools for profiling and analyzing the performance of your algorithms. You can use the built-in profiling tools to identify bottlenecks, memory usage, and CPU usage. This is crucial for optimizing your algorithms and ensuring they run efficiently.

Version Control:

Integrate your algorithm development process with version control using Git. Visual Studio has Git integration that allows you to track changes, collaborate with team members, and manage different versions of your code.

Documentation and Comments:

Use Visual Studio's features to document your code and add comments. Well-documented algorithms are easier to understand and maintain. Intuitive code comments help both you and other developers comprehend the purpose and logic behind your algorithms.

Conclusion:

In this section, we've explored how to leverage Microsoft Visual Studio for algorithm development. Visual Studio's powerful features, including code editing, debugging, profiling, and version control, provide a robust environment for creating, testing, and optimizing algorithms. By using these tools effectively, you can streamline your algorithm development process and create high-quality code that efficiently solves complex problems. As you continue to hone your skills, you'll find Visual Studio to be an invaluable asset in your journey towards mastering data structures and algorithms.

CHAPTER VII
Working with Libraries and Packages

7.1 Managing Dependencies with NuGet

Modern software development often relies on leveraging existing libraries and packages to streamline the development process and avoid reinventing the wheel. Microsoft Visual Studio provides a powerful package management tool called NuGet that makes it easy to manage and incorporate third-party libraries, components, and tools into your projects.

Understanding NuGet:

NuGet is a package manager for .NET and other development platforms. It simplifies the process of discovering, installing, and updating external packages, saving you time and effort. These packages can include libraries, frameworks, tools, and even custom code that you or other developers have created.

Using NuGet in Visual Studio:

1. Open your Visual Studio project.

2. Right-click on the project in the Solution Explorer and select "Manage NuGet Packages..."

3. The NuGet Package Manager window will appear. Here, you can search for packages using keywords, browse different categories, or enter the exact package name you're looking for.

4. Once you find the desired package, select it from the list and click the "Install" button.

5. NuGet will download and add the package to your project, along with any necessary dependencies.

Example: Adding Newtonsoft.Json Library with NuGet

1. Open your Visual Studio project.

2. Right-click on the project in the Solution Explorer and select "Manage NuGet Packages..."

3. In the NuGet Package Manager window, search for "Newtonsoft.Json."

4. Select the "Newtonsoft.Json" package from the search results and click the "Install" button.

5. NuGet will download and add the Newtonsoft.Json library to your project.

Managing Packages via Package Manager Console:

Visual Studio also allows you to manage packages using the Package Manager Console, which provides a command-line interface for NuGet operations.

1. Go to "View" > "Other Windows" > "Package Manager Console."

2. In the Package Manager Console, use commands like `Install-Package`, `Update-Package`, and `Uninstall-Package` to manage packages.

3. For example, to install a package, use the command `Install-Package PackageName`.

Benefits of Using NuGet:

1. Time-Saving: NuGet simplifies the process of adding and managing dependencies, saving you time that you can dedicate to actual development.

2. Version Management: NuGet helps ensure you're using the correct and compatible versions of packages, reducing conflicts and compatibility issues.

3. Community Contributions: Many open-source packages are available on NuGet, created and maintained by a large community of developers.

4. Consistency: NuGet packages can help maintain consistent coding patterns across projects by providing reusable components.

5. Security: NuGet packages are typically vetted and reviewed, which can enhance the security of your applications.

Best Practices:

1. Regular Updates: Periodically update your packages to benefit from bug fixes, enhancements, and security patches.

2. Package Integrity: Only use packages from trusted sources and verify their authenticity before integration.

3. Document Dependencies: Clearly document the external packages and their versions used in your project for future reference.

Conclusion:

Managing dependencies with NuGet in Microsoft Visual Studio is an essential skill for modern software developers. By effectively utilizing NuGet, you can easily incorporate third-party libraries and tools into your projects, enhance your development process, and ensure the quality and security of your applications. As you continue to work with NuGet and expand your knowledge of package management, you'll become more proficient at building robust and efficient software solutions.

7.2. Integrating Third-Party Libraries

In the world of software development, leveraging third-party libraries can significantly accelerate your project's progress and help you achieve complex functionality without reinventing the wheel. Integrating third-party libraries into your Microsoft Visual Studio project is a common practice that can enhance your application's capabilities and reduce development time. In this chapter, we'll explore the process of integrating third-party libraries, including why it's important, how to find and evaluate libraries, and how to seamlessly integrate them into your projects.

Understanding the Importance of Third-Party Libraries:

Third-party libraries are pre-built code modules that provide specific functionalities. They are created and maintained by other developers, often as open-source projects, and can range from simple utilities to complex frameworks. Utilizing these libraries can offer several benefits:

1. Time Efficiency: Leveraging third-party libraries saves time by allowing you to focus on solving unique problems rather than writing basic functionalities.

2. Quality and Reliability: Established libraries are typically well-tested by a broad user base, contributing to the stability and reliability of your application.

3. Functionality: Libraries can provide advanced features and capabilities that might be challenging or time-consuming to implement from scratch.

4. Community Support: Active open-source libraries often have a community of developers providing support, updates, and bug fixes.

Finding and Evaluating Third-Party Libraries:

1. Use a Package Manager: As discussed in the previous section (7.1), NuGet is an excellent tool for discovering and integrating third-party libraries into your Visual Studio projects.

2. Online Resources: Websites like GitHub, NuGet.org, and Stack Overflow are valuable resources for discovering and evaluating libraries. Look for libraries with a strong user base, recent updates, and positive community feedback.

3. Documentation and Usage: Thoroughly review the library's documentation to understand its features, usage instructions, and any potential limitations. Look for examples, tutorials, and code samples.

4. Community Engagement: Check the library's GitHub repository or community forum to gauge the developer's responsiveness to issues and questions.

Integrating Third-Party Libraries:

Integrating a third-party library into your Visual Studio project is generally a straightforward process:

1. Install the Library: Use NuGet to install the desired library into your project. Right-click your project in the Solution Explorer, select "Manage NuGet Packages," search for the library, and click "Install."

2. Import and Use: Once the library is installed, you can import it into your code by adding an appropriate `using` directive (C#) or `import` statement (Python). You can then use the library's classes, methods, and functionalities in your code.

Example: Integrating Newtonsoft.Json Library:

Let's integrate the popular Newtonsoft.Json library for JSON serialization and deserialization in a C# project:

1. Open your Visual Studio project.

2. Right-click on the project in the Solution Explorer and select "Manage NuGet Packages..."

3. Search for "Newtonsoft.Json" and click "Install" to add the library to your project.

4. In your C# code, add the following using directive to start using the library:

```csharp
using Newtonsoft.Json;
```

5. You can now use classes and methods from the Newtonsoft.Json library, such as `JsonConvert.SerializeObject` and `JsonConvert.DeserializeObject`, to work with JSON data.

Benefits and Considerations:

1. Code Modularity: Third-party libraries promote modular code design by allowing you to separate concerns and delegate specific tasks to well-established components.

2. Maintenance: Be mindful of library updates and changes. Regularly update libraries to benefit from bug fixes and new features.

3. License Compatibility: Review the library's licensing terms to ensure they align with your project's requirements.

4. Dependencies: Be aware of the libraries your chosen third-party library depends on. Ensure there are no conflicts with existing dependencies.

Conclusion:

Integrating third-party libraries into your Microsoft Visual Studio projects is a powerful technique that can enhance your application's capabilities, improve development efficiency, and leverage the expertise of the broader developer community. By effectively finding, evaluating, and integrating third-party libraries, you can accelerate your development process, create more robust applications, and ultimately deliver high-quality software solutions to your users.

7.3. Exploring Available Packages

As a software developer, harnessing the power of existing libraries and packages is essential for building robust and feature-rich applications efficiently. In this chapter, we will delve into the process of exploring available packages, understanding how to search for and evaluate them, and effectively incorporating them into your projects within Microsoft Visual Studio.

Why Explore Available Packages:

Exploring available packages allows you to tap into a vast ecosystem of pre-built solutions that can accelerate your development process. By leveraging well-designed and tested packages, you can avoid reinventing the wheel and focus on the unique aspects of your project.

Finding and Exploring Packages:

1. NuGet Package Manager: As mentioned earlier, NuGet is a powerful package manager integrated into Visual Studio. To access it, right-click on your project in the Solution Explorer and select "Manage NuGet Packages." From here, you can browse, search, and install packages.

2. Online Package Repositories: NuGet.org is the default repository for .NET packages, but there are others like npm for JavaScript, PyPI for Python, and Maven for Java. These repositories provide extensive lists of available packages, often accompanied by documentation, usage examples, and user ratings.

Evaluating Packages:

1. Popularity and Community: Packages with a large user base and active community engagement are often safer choices. Look for packages with frequent updates and a history of addressing user issues.

2. Documentation: A well-documented package is easier to understand and integrate. Thorough documentation should provide clear installation instructions, usage guidelines, and code examples.

3. Dependencies: Examine the package's dependencies to ensure they align with your project and don't conflict with existing libraries.

4. Recent Updates: Frequent updates can indicate a package's maintainability and responsiveness to user needs.

Exploring Packages in NuGet:

Let's explore the process of finding and integrating a package using the NuGet Package Manager:

1. Open your Visual Studio project.

2. Right-click on the project in the Solution Explorer and select "Manage NuGet Packages..."

3. In the NuGet Package Manager window, you can search for packages by name, keywords, or functionality.

4. Once you find a suitable package, click on it to view details, documentation, and dependencies.

5. Click the "Install" button to add the package to your project.

Example: Exploring and Installing Newtonsoft.Json Package:

1. Open your Visual Studio project.

2. Right-click on the project in the Solution Explorer and select "Manage NuGet Packages..."

3. Search for "Newtonsoft.Json," a popular JSON serialization/deserialization library for .NET.

4. Click on the package to view details and documentation.

5. Click the "Install" button to integrate the package into your project.

Benefits and Considerations:

1. Time Efficiency: Exploring available packages saves you time by providing solutions for common tasks.

2. Code Quality: Well-maintained packages offer tested and optimized solutions, enhancing your application's overall quality.

3. Community Support: Utilizing popular packages connects you with a community of developers who can provide assistance and guidance.

Conclusion:

Exploring available packages is an integral part of modern software development. By effectively utilizing package managers like NuGet and exploring online repositories, you can quickly discover, evaluate, and integrate powerful solutions into your Microsoft Visual Studio projects. The ability to leverage existing packages empowers you to build innovative and efficient applications while benefiting from the collective expertise of the developer community.

CHAPTER VIII
Introduction to Web Development in Visual Studio

8.1 Creating a Basic HTML Page

In today's digital age, web development is a fundamental skill for software developers. Microsoft Visual Studio provides a powerful environment for creating web applications, and in this chapter, we'll dive into the basics of web development using Visual Studio by creating a simple HTML page.

Why Learn HTML and Web Development:

HTML (Hypertext Markup Language) is the building block of web pages. Understanding HTML is essential for anyone looking to create and design web content. Web development skills are in high demand as businesses and individuals continue to establish an online presence.

Creating a Basic HTML Page:

Creating a basic HTML page involves defining the structure and content of the web page. Let's go through the steps to create a simple HTML page using Visual Studio:

1. Open Visual Studio:

Launch Microsoft Visual Studio and ensure you have a project open or create a new project.

2. Add a New HTML File:

Right-click on the project in the Solution Explorer, navigate to "Add" > "New Item," and select "HTML Page." Give the file a name, such as "index.html," and click "Add."

3. Edit the HTML Content:

Double-click on the newly created HTML file to open it in the code editor. You'll see a basic HTML structure with `<html>`, `<head>`, and `<body>` tags. Modify the content within the `<body>` tag to create your web page.

Example:

```html
<!DOCTYPE html>
<html>
<head>
    <title>My First Web Page</title>
</head>
<body>
    <h1>Hello, World!</h1>
    <p>This is a basic HTML page created in Visual Studio.</p>
</body>
</html>
```

4. Preview the HTML Page:

To preview your HTML page, right-click on the HTML file in the Solution Explorer and select "View in Browser" or simply press `Ctrl+F5`.

Enhancing Your HTML Page:

Once you have created a basic HTML page, you can enhance it by adding additional HTML elements, CSS styling, and JavaScript functionality. Here are a few ideas to consider:

1. CSS Styling: Use the `<style>` tag or an external CSS file to add styles and layout to your HTML elements.

2. Images and Links: Insert images using the `<img>` tag and create hyperlinks with the `<a>` tag.

3. Lists and Tables: Create ordered or unordered lists using the `<ul>` and `<ol>` tags, and format data with HTML tables.

Conclusion:

Creating a basic HTML page is the first step in your journey into web development with Microsoft Visual Studio. Understanding HTML is essential for building and structuring web content, and Visual Studio provides a convenient platform for writing, editing, and previewing HTML code. As you become more comfortable with HTML, you can explore additional web development technologies and tools to create dynamic and interactive web applications.

8.2. Styling with CSS

Cascading Style Sheets (CSS) is a fundamental technology in web development that allows you to control the presentation and layout of HTML elements on a web page. In this section, we will explore how to style your HTML content using CSS within Microsoft Visual Studio.

Why Use CSS:

CSS provides the means to separate the design and layout of a web page from its content. By using CSS, you can achieve consistent styling across your entire website, making it visually appealing and user-friendly.

Styling with CSS in Visual Studio:

Here's how you can apply CSS styles to your HTML elements using Visual Studio:

1. Open Your HTML File:

Ensure you have an HTML file open in Visual Studio, such as the "index.html" file created in the previous chapter.

2. Add a `<style>` Section:

Within the `<head>` section of your HTML file, add a `<style>` tag to define your CSS rules. You can also link to an external CSS file using the `<link>` tag.

Example:
```html
<!DOCTYPE html>
<html>
<head>
   <title>My Stylish Web Page</title>
   <style>
      /* CSS rules go here */
```

```
    </style>
  </head>
  <body>
    <!-- HTML content goes here -->
  </body>
</html>
```

3. Apply Styles to HTML Elements:

Inside the `<style>` section, you can define CSS rules to target specific HTML elements. Use selectors to specify which elements you want to style and apply various properties to control their appearance.

Example:
```css
/* CSS rules for styling */
body {
    font-family: Arial, sans-serif;
    background-color: #f2f2f2;
}
h1 {
    color: blue;
}
p {
    font-size: 16px;
```

```
}

```
```
```

4. Preview Your Styled Page:

Save your HTML file and preview it in a web browser to see the applied styles. Right-click on the HTML file in the Solution Explorer and select "View in Browser" or press `Ctrl+F5`.

Enhancing Styling with CSS:

As you become more familiar with CSS, you can explore advanced styling techniques, including:

1. CSS Classes and IDs: Use classes and IDs to apply styles to specific elements, giving you more control over individual elements.

2. Box Model and Layout: Learn about the box model to control element dimensions, margins, borders, and padding. Use CSS properties like `margin`, `padding`, `width`, and `height`.

3. Responsive Design: Implement responsive design principles to ensure your web page looks good on various screen sizes and devices.

Conclusion:

Styling with CSS is an essential skill in web development, and Microsoft Visual Studio makes it easy to apply styles to your HTML elements. By using CSS, you can enhance the visual appeal of your web pages and create a consistent and professional-looking website. As you continue to learn and experiment with CSS, you'll have the power to transform your HTML content into engaging and visually pleasing web experiences.

8.3. Adding Interactivity with JavaScript

JavaScript is a versatile programming language that adds interactivity and dynamic behavior to your web pages. In this section, we will explore how to incorporate JavaScript into your web development projects using Microsoft Visual Studio.

Why Use JavaScript:

JavaScript allows you to create responsive and interactive web pages that respond to user actions, such as clicking buttons, filling out forms, and more. It enables you to manipulate the Document Object Model (DOM) to dynamically update and modify the content and behavior of your web pages.

Adding JavaScript to Your Web Page:

Here's how you can add JavaScript code to your HTML page using Visual Studio:

1. Open Your HTML File:

Ensure you have an HTML file open in Visual Studio, such as the "index.html" file we've been working on.

2. Create a `<script>` Tag:

Inside the `<body>` section of your HTML file, add a `<script>` tag to include your JavaScript code. You can also link to an external JavaScript file using the `<script>` tag's `src` attribute.

Example:

```html
```

```html
<!DOCTYPE html>
<html>
<head>
    <title>Interactive Web Page</title>
</head>
<body>
    <!-- HTML content goes here -->


    <!-- Include JavaScript -->
    <script>
        // Your JavaScript code goes here
    </script>
</body>
</html>
```

3. Writing JavaScript Code:

Inside the `<script>` tag, write your JavaScript code. You can create functions, manipulate the DOM, and respond to events such as button clicks.

Example:

```javascript
// JavaScript code for interactivity
function showMessage() {
    alert('Hello, this is an interactive message!');
```

}

```
```

4. Using JavaScript to Enhance Interactivity:

You can use JavaScript to perform various tasks, such as:

- **Event Handling:** Attach event listeners to HTML elements to respond to user actions.

- **DOM Manipulation:** Modify the content and structure of your web page on the fly.

- **Form Validation:** Validate user input in forms before submitting data to the server.

- **AJAX:** Perform asynchronous requests to fetch or send data to the server without refreshing the page.

5. Testing Your JavaScript Code:

Save your HTML file and open it in a web browser to see your JavaScript code in action. You can use the browser's developer tools to debug and inspect your JavaScript code.

Exploring JavaScript Frameworks:

As you become more comfortable with JavaScript, you can explore popular JavaScript frameworks and libraries, such as jQuery, React, and Vue.js. These frameworks provide additional tools and components for building complex and interactive web applications.

Conclusion:

Adding interactivity with JavaScript is a crucial aspect of modern web development. Microsoft Visual Studio provides a convenient environment for writing and testing JavaScript code alongside your HTML and CSS. By incorporating JavaScript into your web projects, you can create engaging and dynamic user experiences that respond to user interactions and make your web pages more interactive and user-friendly. As you continue to learn and experiment with JavaScript, you'll unlock the full potential of web development and create web applications that delight users and provide valuable functionality.

CHAPTER IX
Building and Testing APIs

9.1 Creating a RESTful API

Application Programming Interfaces (APIs) serve as the backbone of modern software applications, enabling communication and interaction between different systems. In this chapter, we will delve into the process of creating a RESTful API using Microsoft Visual Studio, a crucial skill for web developers.

Understanding RESTful APIs:

A RESTful API (Representational State Transfer) is an architectural style for designing networked applications. It follows a set of principles and constraints to ensure a standardized way of interacting with resources over HTTP. RESTful APIs use HTTP methods (GET, POST, PUT, DELETE) to perform operations on resources, and responses are typically in JSON or XML format.

Creating a RESTful API with Visual Studio:

Here's a step-by-step guide on creating a simple RESTful API using Visual Studio:

1. Open Visual Studio:

Launch Microsoft Visual Studio and create a new project. Choose the appropriate project template for your preferred programming language (such as C#).

2. Create a New Web API Project:

Select the "Web API" template from the available project templates. This template is designed to create a project with the necessary structure for building APIs.

3. Define Your API Controller:

In your project, you will find a "Controllers" folder. Right-click on it and choose "Add" > "Controller." Select the "API Controller - Empty" template. Give your controller a name, such as "ProductsController."

4. Implement API Endpoints:

Inside your API controller, define methods for various HTTP methods (GET, POST, PUT, DELETE) to handle different API endpoints. For example:

```csharp
[Route("api/[controller]")]

[ApiController]

public class ProductsController : ControllerBase

{

    // GET api/products

    [HttpGet]

    public ActionResult<IEnumerable<string>> Get()

    {

        // Retrieve and return data

    }


    // POST api/products

    [HttpPost]
```

```csharp
public ActionResult<string> Post([FromBody] Product product)
{
    // Create a new product
}


// PUT api/products/5
[HttpPut("{id}")]
public ActionResult<string> Put(int id, [FromBody] Product product)
{
    // Update the product with the specified ID
}


// DELETE api/products/5
[HttpDelete("{id}")]
public ActionResult<string> Delete(int id)
{
    // Delete the product with the specified ID
}
}
```
```

## 5. Configure Routing:

Make sure you have configured the routing correctly in the `Startup.cs` file to map your API endpoints to the appropriate controller actions.
```

6. Testing Your API:

Run your project, and your API will be accessible at URLs like `https://localhost:port/api/products`. You can use tools like Postman or browser extensions to send requests to your API endpoints and verify their functionality.

Adding Data Persistence:

For a real-world scenario, you would likely want to store and retrieve data from a database. You can integrate Entity Framework to manage data operations within your API.

Conclusion:

Creating a RESTful API is a fundamental skill for web developers, allowing them to expose data and functionality to other applications. Microsoft Visual Studio streamlines the process of building APIs by providing project templates and tools for handling HTTP requests and responses. By mastering the art of creating APIs, you can empower your applications to communicate effectively with other systems, making your software more versatile and interoperable.

9.2. Testing APIs with Postman

API testing is a critical part of the software development process, ensuring that your APIs are functioning correctly and producing the expected results. Postman is a powerful tool that simplifies the process of testing APIs by providing a user-friendly interface to create and execute API requests, monitor responses, and automate testing scenarios. In this chapter, we will explore how to use Postman for testing APIs.

Getting Started with Postman:

1. Download and Install Postman:

First, download and install Postman from the official website (https://www.postman.com/downloads/). Postman is available for various operating systems, including Windows, macOS, and Linux.

2. Launch Postman:

After installation, launch the Postman application.

Creating API Requests:

1. Create a New Request:

In Postman, you can create a new request by clicking the "New" button and selecting "Request."

2. Enter Request Details:

Provide the request's name and description for better organization. Choose the HTTP method (GET, POST, PUT, DELETE) you want to test.

3. Enter Request URL:

Enter the URL of the API endpoint you want to test. For example, if you are testing a "GET" request for a list of products, the URL might be "https://api.example.com/products."

4. Add Headers and Parameters:

If your API requires headers or query parameters, you can add them in the respective sections.

5. Send the Request:

Click the "Send" button to execute the request. Postman will display the response, including the status code, headers, and body.

Working with Responses:

1. Inspecting Response Details:

Postman provides a detailed view of the API response, including the response body, headers, and status code. This allows you to verify that the API is returning the expected data.

2. Validating Response Data:

You can use Postman's built-in validation features to verify that the response data matches the expected format and values. For example, you can check if a specific field exists or has a certain value.

Automating API Testing:

1. Creating Test Suites:

Postman allows you to organize multiple API requests into test suites. This is particularly useful for testing different scenarios or endpoints together.

2. Writing Tests:

You can write tests using JavaScript to automate the validation of API responses. For instance, you can check if the response status code is 200, or if a specific field contains the expected value.

3. Running Collections:

A collection is a group of requests and tests. You can create collections in Postman and run them to automate testing workflows.

Advanced Features:

1. Environment Variables:

Postman lets you define environment variables, making it easy to switch between different environments (e.g., development, production) without modifying requests.

2. Data-Driven Testing:

You can use CSV files or data files to perform data-driven testing, sending multiple requests with different data sets.

Conclusion:

Testing APIs with Postman is an essential part of the development process. It enables developers to ensure the reliability and correctness of their APIs, leading to more robust and stable applications. With its user-friendly interface and powerful features, Postman simplifies the task of creating, executing, and automating API tests, ultimately contributing to the overall quality of your software projects.

9.3. Documenting Your API

API documentation plays a crucial role in helping developers understand how to use your API effectively. Well-documented APIs make it easier for other developers to integrate with your services, leading to better adoption and collaboration. In this chapter, we will explore the importance of API documentation and how to effectively document your API using tools like Swagger.

The Importance of API Documentation:

Clear and comprehensive API documentation offers several benefits:

1. Ease of Integration: Documentation provides clear instructions on how to use endpoints, parameters, authentication, and response formats, making integration smoother.

2. Reduced Learning Curve: Developers can quickly understand how to interact with your API without spending excessive time experimenting.

3. Error Handling: Properly documented error codes and messages help developers troubleshoot issues effectively.

4. Consistency: Documentation ensures that all developers use the API in a standardized way, reducing confusion and potential errors.

Documenting Your API:

1. Choose a Documentation Tool:

One popular tool for documenting APIs is Swagger, now known as OpenAPI. It provides a standardized format for describing APIs, making it easier for developers to understand and use them.

2. Integrate Swagger into Your API:

Start by integrating the Swagger/OpenAPI specification into your API codebase. This involves adding annotations or comments to your code to describe endpoints, request/response formats, and authentication.

3. Generate Documentation:

Once your API is annotated with Swagger/OpenAPI specifications, you can use tools like Swashbuckle (for .NET) or Swagger UI to automatically generate interactive documentation. This documentation will include details about each endpoint, request parameters, response formats, and sample requests.

Documenting Endpoints:

1. Describe Endpoints:

For each endpoint, provide a clear and concise description of its purpose, expected behavior, and the data it manipulates.

2. List Parameters:

Specify the parameters the endpoint accepts (query, path, header, body) and their expected formats.

3. Detail Authentication:

If authentication is required, explain how to include authentication tokens or API keys in requests.

4. Response Formats:

Describe the possible response formats (JSON, XML) and provide examples of both successful and error responses.

Interactive Documentation:

1. Swagger UI:

Swagger UI generates a user-friendly interface where developers can explore your API. It allows them to make test requests directly within the documentation and see the responses.

2. Try It Out:

Many interactive documentation tools, including Swagger UI, offer a "Try it out" feature. Users can input parameters, execute requests, and see the actual API responses directly in the documentation.

Best Practices for Effective API Documentation:

1. Use Clear Language: Write documentation in a clear and concise manner, avoiding jargon. Use simple language to explain complex concepts.

2. Provide Examples: Include detailed examples for various API requests and responses. These examples help developers understand the expected data formats.

3. Include Code Samples: Offer code snippets in multiple programming languages to demonstrate how to use your API.

4. Update Regularly: Keep your documentation up to date as you make changes to your API. Outdated documentation can lead to confusion and errors.

Conclusion:

Documenting your API is an essential step in ensuring its usability and adoption. Properly documented APIs empower developers to integrate with your services more efficiently, leading to better collaboration and successful projects. By using tools like Swagger and following best practices, you can create clear, comprehensive, and interactive documentation that benefits both developers and end-users.

CHAPTER X
Deployment and Publishing

10.1 Preparing Your Application for Deployment

Deploying your application is a crucial step in making it available to users. Before you can publish your application, there are several important considerations and steps to take to ensure a smooth and successful deployment process. This chapter will guide you through the process of preparing your application for deployment, covering essential aspects such as environment configuration, optimizing performance, and handling dependencies.

Understanding Deployment Preparation:

Before you start the deployment process, it's important to ensure that your application is ready for production use. This involves tasks such as:

1. Environment Configuration: Ensure that your application is configured to run in the target production environment. This includes setting up connection strings, environment variables, and other configuration settings.

2. Performance Optimization: Optimize your application's performance to ensure it can handle production-level traffic. This might involve optimizing database queries, caching data, and minimizing resource-intensive operations.

3. Security: Review your application's security measures, including data encryption, authentication, and authorization. Make sure that sensitive information is properly protected.

4. Error Handling and Logging: Implement robust error handling and logging mechanisms to capture and diagnose errors that may occur in the production environment.

Dependency Management:

1. Update Dependencies: Ensure that all third-party libraries and packages your application depends on are up to date. Outdated dependencies can lead to security vulnerabilities and compatibility issues.

2. Check Licenses: Review the licenses of the libraries and packages you're using to ensure compliance. Some licenses may have restrictions that could impact your application's usage.

Testing and Quality Assurance:

1. Testing: Thoroughly test your application before deployment. This includes unit testing, integration testing, and end-to-end testing to identify and fix any issues.

2. Staging Environment: Consider deploying your application to a staging or testing environment that closely mirrors the production environment. This allows you to identify and address any deployment-related issues before they impact users.

Database Preparation:

1. Schema Changes: If your application uses a database, ensure that any necessary schema changes are applied. Use database migration tools to manage schema changes across different environments.

2. Data Migration: If you're deploying updates to an existing application, plan for data migration strategies to ensure that existing data is properly migrated to the new version.

Configuration Management:

1. Environment-specific Configuration: Use configuration management techniques to handle environment-specific settings. This allows you to easily switch between development, testing, and production configurations.

2. Secret Management: Safely manage sensitive information such as API keys, passwords, and tokens. Avoid hardcoding these values in your code and use environment variables or secret management tools.

Deployment Scripts and Automation:

1. Deployment Scripts: Create deployment scripts or automation workflows to streamline the deployment process. Tools like Azure DevOps, Jenkins, or GitHub Actions can help automate deployment tasks.

2. Rollback Plan: Have a rollback plan in place in case something goes wrong during deployment. This ensures that you can quickly revert to a stable version of your application.

Documentation:

1. Deployment Guide: Create a deployment guide that outlines the steps required to deploy the application. This guide should include detailed instructions and any prerequisites.

2. Troubleshooting: Provide troubleshooting tips and common solutions for deployment-related issues that may arise.

Conclusion:

Preparing your application for deployment is a critical step in ensuring its successful launch and operation in a production environment. By addressing environment configuration, performance optimization, dependency management, and other key considerations, you can increase the chances of a smooth deployment process and provide users with a reliable and high-quality experience.

10.2. Publishing Your Application

Publishing your application is the final step in the deployment process, making your software accessible to users on the internet or within your organization. This chapter focuses on the practical aspects of publishing an application, guiding you through the steps required to deploy your code, assets, and configurations to a production environment.

Understanding Application Publishing:

Publishing an application involves making it available for users to access and interact with. Depending on the type of application and your target audience, the publishing process may vary. Here, we'll explore a general process for publishing web applications.

1. Choose a Hosting Provider:

Select a hosting provider that suits your application's requirements. Common options include cloud platforms like Azure, AWS, or Google Cloud, as well as traditional web hosts.

2. Prepare Your Application:

Before publishing, ensure that your application is ready for production. This includes thoroughly testing the application, optimizing its performance, and resolving any outstanding issues.

3. Configure the Hosting Environment:

Configure your hosting environment to support your application's technology stack. This may involve setting up web servers, databases, and other necessary infrastructure.

4. Publishing Options:

Depending on your application type, you have several options for publishing:

a. Web Applications:

- **FTP/SFTP:** If using a traditional host, you can use File Transfer Protocol (FTP) or Secure FTP (SFTP) to upload your files to the server.

- **Deployment Scripts:** For more complex scenarios, consider using deployment scripts or automation tools like Azure DevOps Pipelines or GitHub Actions to automate the deployment process.

b. Cloud Platforms:

- **Platform as a Service (PaaS):** Cloud platforms like Azure App Service or AWS Elastic Beanstalk provide PaaS solutions that simplify the deployment process.

- Containerization: Package your application into containers using technologies like Docker and deploy them on container orchestration platforms like Kubernetes.

5. Configuration and Settings:

Configure environment-specific settings, connection strings, and other configuration options required for your application to run correctly in the production environment.

6. Security Measures:

Implement necessary security measures, such as setting up firewalls, securing APIs, and enabling HTTPS for secure data transmission.

7. Deploy Your Application:

Follow these general steps to deploy your application:

a. Traditional Hosting:

1. Access your hosting account via FTP/SFTP or a control panel provided by your host.

2. Upload your application files and assets to the server.

3. Configure domain settings (DNS) to point to the server's IP address.

b. Cloud Platforms:

1. Use deployment scripts or automation tools to package and deploy your application to the cloud platform.

2. Configure routing and scaling settings as needed.

3. Associate a custom domain or subdomain with your application.

8. Testing and Verification:

After deployment, thoroughly test your application in the production environment to ensure everything is working as expected. Test functionality, performance, and responsiveness.

9. Monitoring and Maintenance:

Implement monitoring tools and strategies to keep track of your application's health and performance. Set up alerts for potential issues and perform regular maintenance.

10. Continuous Deployment:

Consider setting up continuous deployment practices to automate future updates and ensure a smooth deployment process for future releases.

Conclusion:

Publishing your application marks the culmination of your development efforts. By following the steps outlined in this chapter and tailoring them to your specific application and hosting environment, you can confidently deploy your software to a production setting and provide users with access to your valuable creation. Remember that the deployment process may differ based on your application's requirements and the chosen hosting platform, so be sure to refer to the platform's documentation for specific instructions.

10.3. Continuous Integration/Continuous Deployment (CI/CD) with Visual Studio

Continuous Integration/Continuous Deployment (CI/CD) is a software development practice that aims to automate and streamline the process of building, testing, and deploying applications. It enhances the development workflow by ensuring that code changes are automatically validated and deployed to production or staging environments, reducing manual intervention and minimizing the risk of errors. In this chapter, we will explore how to implement CI/CD pipelines for your applications using Visual Studio and related tools.

Understanding CI/CD:

CI/CD is a crucial part of modern software development that promotes collaboration, reliability, and faster release cycles. It consists of two main components:

1. Continuous Integration (CI): Developers frequently merge their code changes into a shared repository. Each integration triggers automated build and test processes to detect integration issues early.

2. Continuous Deployment (CD): Automated deployment processes ensure that validated code changes are automatically deployed to production or staging environments.

Benefits of CI/CD:

- Faster Development Cycles: CI/CD accelerates the development process by automating build, test, and deployment tasks.

- Early Issue Detection: Automated tests catch bugs and integration issues early, reducing the effort required for debugging.

- Consistency: Automation ensures that deployments are consistent across different environments.

- Reduced Risk: Automated testing and deployment reduce the risk of human error and deployment failures.

- Quick Rollback: In case of issues, CI/CD allows for quick rollback to a known working state.

Implementing CI/CD with Visual Studio:

Visual Studio provides tools and integrations to set up CI/CD pipelines for your applications. Here's a step-by-step guide to implementing CI/CD using Visual Studio and Azure DevOps:

1. Setting Up Source Control:

Ensure your application code is stored in a version control system, such as Git, which allows for collaboration and version management.

2. Creating a CI/CD Pipeline:

1. Azure DevOps: Create a new project in Azure DevOps and set up a new CI/CD pipeline.

2. Pipeline Configuration: Configure your pipeline to trigger on code commits to the specified repository.

3. Build Stage: Define a build stage to compile your code and run automated tests.

4. Artifact Publishing: Publish build artifacts to a location accessible by the deployment stage.

3. Setting Up Deployment:

1. Deployment Environment: Define the target deployment environment, which can be a testing or production environment.

2. Deployment Stage: Configure a deployment stage in your pipeline.

3. Deployment Tasks: Define tasks for deploying your application, such as copying files, setting up configurations, and more.

4. Continuous Monitoring:

1. Automated Tests: Integrate automated testing into your pipeline to ensure code quality.

2. Integration Tests: Perform integration tests to validate the application in the deployment environment.

3. Manual Approval: Add a manual approval step before deploying to production to ensure quality control.

5. Rollback Plan:

Define a rollback plan in case deployment issues arise. This can involve automated rollback tasks or a documented manual process.

6. Monitoring and Alerts:

Integrate monitoring tools to track the health and performance of your deployed application. Set up alerts for any anomalies.

7. Iterative Improvement:

Regularly review and refine your CI/CD pipeline to incorporate feedback and make necessary improvements.

Example Workflow:

1. Developer A pushes code changes to the repository.

2. CI/CD pipeline automatically triggers a build and runs tests.

3. If tests pass, the pipeline deploys the application to the staging environment.

4. Automated tests run in the staging environment.

5. Upon successful tests, a manual approval step is required for deploying to production.

6. After approval, the pipeline deploys the application to the production environment.

Conclusion:

Implementing CI/CD with Visual Studio and Azure DevOps streamlines your development process, improves code quality, and ensures consistent and reliable deployments. By automating build, test, and deployment tasks, you can focus on writing code and delivering value to users, while also reducing the risk of errors and improving collaboration among your development team.

CHAPTER XI
Collaborative Coding with Visual Studio

11.1 Working in Teams with Visual Studio

In today's software development landscape, teamwork and collaboration are essential for building complex and high-quality applications. Visual Studio provides a range of features and tools that enable developers to work together efficiently in a team environment. In this chapter, we will explore how to leverage Visual Studio's collaborative capabilities to enhance teamwork, streamline code sharing, and improve code quality.

Understanding Collaborative Coding:

Collaborative coding involves multiple developers working together on the same project, contributing code, and sharing updates seamlessly. This approach offers several benefits:

1. Efficient Code Sharing: Developers can easily share their code changes with others, facilitating faster integration.

2. Real-time Collaboration: Multiple developers can work on the same codebase simultaneously, seeing each other's changes in real-time.

3. Reduced Conflicts: Collaboration tools help identify and resolve code conflicts early, minimizing integration issues.

4. Code Review: Team members can review each other's code, leading to improved code quality and knowledge sharing.

Visual Studio Tools for Collaborative Coding:

Visual Studio offers a range of features and integrations that support collaborative coding:

1. Git Integration: Visual Studio's built-in Git integration allows developers to clone repositories, create branches, commit changes, and manage pull requests seamlessly.

2. Code Reviews: Visual Studio provides tools for conducting code reviews within the IDE. Developers can add comments, suggest changes, and approve code before merging.

3. Live Share: The Live Share extension enables real-time collaboration by allowing developers to share their code and collaborate with others in the same coding session.

4. Azure DevOps Integration: Visual Studio integrates with Azure DevOps for managing work items, tracking progress, and automating build and deployment pipelines.

5. CodeLens: CodeLens provides insights into code changes, references, and authors directly within the code editor, enhancing code understanding.

Best Practices for Collaborative Coding:

To ensure effective collaboration in a team environment, consider the following best practices:

1. Use Version Control: Leverage Git or other version control systems to manage code changes, branches, and pull requests.

2. Branching Strategy: Adopt a branching strategy that suits your team's workflow. Common strategies include feature branching, Gitflow, and trunk-based development.

3. Code Review: Encourage regular code reviews to maintain code quality and share knowledge among team members.

4. Communication: Establish clear communication channels for discussing code changes, addressing issues, and sharing updates.

5. Coding Standards: Define coding standards and guidelines to ensure consistency across the codebase.

6. Automated Testing: Implement automated testing to catch bugs and issues early in the development process.

Example Scenario: Collaborative Feature Development:

1. Developer A creates a new feature branch from the main repository using Visual Studio's Git integration.

2. Developer A implements the feature, commits changes, and pushes them to the remote repository.

3. Developer B reviews the changes using Visual Studio's code review tools, adds comments, and suggests improvements.

4. Developer A and B address the review comments and finalize the changes.

5. Developers A and B use Live Share to collaborate in real-time, making further improvements together.

6. The feature branch is merged into the main repository after passing automated tests and receiving approvals.

Conclusion:

Collaborative coding with Visual Studio empowers development teams to work together efficiently, produce high-quality code, and deliver projects successfully. By leveraging features like Git integration, code reviews, and Live Share, developers can seamlessly collaborate on codebases, share knowledge, and build robust software solutions. Adhering to best practices and effective communication ensures smooth collaboration and contributes to the overall success of the team's projects.

11.2. Code Review and Collaboration Tools

Effective code review and collaboration are critical components of modern software development. They help improve code quality, catch bugs early, share knowledge among team members, and ensure that the final product meets the desired standards. Visual Studio offers a range of powerful tools and features that facilitate code review and collaboration within your development team. In this chapter, we will explore these tools and learn how to leverage them for efficient and productive collaborative coding.

Understanding Code Review and Collaboration:

Code review is the process of examining code changes made by one developer and having them reviewed by other team members. It ensures that the code is well-written, follows coding standards, and is free of errors. Effective collaboration, on the other hand, involves seamless communication and interaction among team members during the development process.

Code Review Tools in Visual Studio:

Visual Studio provides several tools that simplify and enhance the code review process:

1. Pull Requests: Visual Studio integrates with Git repositories and popular platforms like GitHub and Azure DevOps. You can create pull requests directly within the IDE, allowing team members to review code changes, comment, suggest improvements, and approve merges.

2. Code Reviews: Within Visual Studio, you can initiate and participate in code reviews. The code review feature provides a dedicated interface for discussing code changes, addressing concerns, and providing feedback.

3. CodeLens: CodeLens displays valuable information about code changes directly within the code editor. It shows who last modified a line of code, when the change was made, and any associated work items or pull requests.

Collaboration Tools in Visual Studio:

Visual Studio also offers tools that support collaboration among developers:

1. Live Share: Live Share allows developers to collaborate in real-time by sharing their code environment. Team members can edit code together, debug collaboratively, and conduct code reviews in real-time.

2. Comments and Discussions: Developers can add comments to specific lines of code, discussing potential improvements, issues, or questions. This promotes ongoing communication and knowledge sharing.

3. Screen Sharing: Visual Studio allows screen sharing during debugging sessions, enabling team members to see and understand the debugging process.

Best Practices for Code Review and Collaboration:

To make the most of code review and collaboration tools in Visual Studio, consider the following best practices:

1. Establish Guidelines: Define clear code review guidelines and standards that team members should follow.

2. Regular Reviews: Encourage frequent code reviews to catch issues early and ensure code quality.

3. Constructive Feedback: Provide constructive feedback during code reviews, focusing on improvements rather than criticisms.

4. Use Annotations: Leverage annotations and comments within the code editor to highlight areas for improvement.

5. Real-time Collaboration: Utilize Live Share for real-time collaboration, especially for complex problem-solving or paired programming.

Example Scenario: Conducting a Code Review:

1. Developer A creates a pull request for a new feature branch on GitHub.

2. Developer B receives a notification in Visual Studio about the pull request and opens it.

3. Developer B reviews the code changes, adds comments to lines of code that need improvement, and suggests changes.

4. Developer A receives the feedback, addresses the comments, and updates the pull request.

5. Developer B approves the changes after reviewing the updated code.

6. The pull request is merged into the main branch.

Conclusion:

Code review and collaboration tools in Visual Studio play a pivotal role in maintaining code quality, fostering teamwork, and ensuring the success of software projects. By utilizing pull requests, code reviews, Live Share, and other features, development teams can effectively collaborate, share knowledge, and collectively work towards building robust and reliable software solutions. Adhering to best practices and open communication ensures that code review and collaboration become integral parts of the development process, resulting in better code, fewer errors, and improved project outcomes.

11.3. Managing Pull Requests and Code Merging

In the world of collaborative software development, managing pull requests and effectively merging code changes are essential tasks. Pull requests provide a structured way to propose and review code changes before they are merged into the main codebase. Merging, on the other hand, involves integrating these changes into the target branch while ensuring code quality and maintaining the integrity of the project. In this chapter, we will delve into the process of managing pull requests and performing code merging using Visual Studio.

Understanding Pull Requests:

A pull request (PR) is a formal request to merge code changes from one branch (usually a feature or bug-fix branch) into another (typically the main branch). Pull requests are used to initiate code review, allowing team members to discuss changes, provide feedback, and ensure that the proposed code changes adhere to coding standards and project requirements.

Creating a Pull Request:

1. Step 1: Create a New Branch: Before making changes, create a new branch from the main branch. This keeps your changes isolated from the main codebase until they are reviewed and approved.

2. Step 2: Make Code Changes: Write your code changes in the new branch, focusing on the specific task or feature.

3. Step 3: Push to Remote: Push your branch to the remote repository (e.g., GitHub or Azure DevOps).

4. Step 4: Open Pull Request: In Visual Studio, navigate to the repository and create a pull request. Choose the source and target branches, provide a title and description, and initiate the pull request.

Reviewing and Approving Pull Requests:

1. Step 1: Review Changes: Team members can review the code changes in the pull request. They can add comments, suggestions, and feedback directly in the pull request interface.

2. Step 2: Address Feedback: The developer who opened the pull request can address the feedback by making necessary changes and pushing them to the same branch.

3. Step 3: Review Iterations: The review process may involve several iterations until the changes are approved and meet the project's standards.

4. Step 4: Approve and Merge: Once the pull request is approved, it can be merged into the target branch. Visual Studio provides a merge button within the pull request interface.

Code Merging Strategies:

Merging code requires careful consideration to avoid conflicts and maintain a stable codebase. Here are some merging strategies:

1. Fast-Forward Merge: When there are no new changes in the target branch, the source branch's changes are applied directly (fast-forwarded).

2. Merge Commit: A merge commit is created to merge changes. This helps preserve the history of both branches.

3. Rebase and Merge: Rebase the source branch onto the target branch, creating a linear history. Then, perform a fast-forward merge.

Conflicts and Resolution:

Conflicts can occur when changes in the source branch overlap with changes in the target branch. Visual Studio's merge tool helps resolve conflicts by allowing you to compare and choose between conflicting changes.

Example Scenario: Managing a Pull Request:

1. Developer A creates a new branch for a bug fix.

2. Developer A makes code changes and opens a pull request to merge into the main branch.

3. Developer B reviews the pull request, suggests some improvements, and asks for clarification on a specific code block.

4. Developer A addresses the feedback by making changes and replying to the comments.

5. Developer B approves the pull request after confirming that the changes meet the project's requirements.

6. Developer A chooses the merge strategy and merges the pull request.

Conclusion:

Effectively managing pull requests and performing code merging are essential skills for collaborative coding. Visual Studio streamlines this process by providing a comprehensive interface for creating, reviewing, and approving pull requests, as well as resolving conflicts and performing merges. By following best practices, ensuring thorough code reviews, and maintaining clear communication among team members, development teams can confidently manage pull requests and code merging, leading to a smoother and more efficient software development lifecycle.elcome

CHAPTER XII
Beyond the Basics: Advanced Features and Resources

12.1 Exploring Advanced Visual Studio Features

As you become more proficient in using Microsoft Visual Studio, you'll discover a range of advanced features and tools that can significantly enhance your development workflow. In this chapter, we will delve into some of these advanced features, showcasing their benefits and providing guidance on how to leverage them effectively.

1. Code Snippets:

Code snippets are pre-defined code blocks that can be easily inserted into your code. They're immensely helpful for writing repetitive code quickly and maintaining consistent coding patterns. To use code snippets:

  - In Visual Studio, type the snippet shortcut (e.g., `for` for a loop) and press Tab twice.

  - The snippet expands, allowing you to fill in placeholders and navigate through them with Tab.

2. Code Analysis Tools:

Visual Studio offers powerful static code analysis tools that help identify potential issues in your codebase. To use code analysis:

  - Right-click on your project in the Solution Explorer.

  - Select "Run Code Analysis" to analyze your code for various code quality and performance issues.

  - Review the analysis results in the Error List window and make necessary improvements.

3. Code Refactoring:

Refactoring tools in Visual Studio allow you to improve the structure and readability of your code without changing its functionality. To perform code refactoring:

- Right-click on a code element (e.g., method, class) and select "Refactor."

- Choose from a range of refactoring options, such as renaming, extracting methods, and more.

4. IntelliTrace:

IntelliTrace is a debugging tool that records and plays back program execution. This can be immensely helpful in diagnosing complex issues. To use IntelliTrace:

- Enable IntelliTrace in the Debug menu.

- Run your application in debugging mode.

- If an issue occurs, you can step back through the execution history to identify the root cause.

5. Performance Profiling:

Visual Studio's performance profiling tools help identify bottlenecks and optimize your application's performance. To profile your application:

- Select "Profile" from the Debug menu.

- Choose a profiling type (CPU, memory, etc.) and start your application.

- Review the profiling results to identify areas for optimization.

6. Azure DevOps Integration:

Visual Studio seamlessly integrates with Azure DevOps (formerly known as Visual Studio Team Services), providing a comprehensive set of tools for version control, continuous integration, and more. To integrate with Azure DevOps:

- Connect your project to an Azure DevOps repository.

- Use features like version control, work items, build pipelines, and release management directly within Visual Studio.

7. Extensions and Marketplace:

Visual Studio has a rich ecosystem of extensions available through the Visual Studio Marketplace. These extensions can enhance your development environment with additional features, languages, and tools. To explore and install extensions:

- Navigate to the Extensions menu in Visual Studio.

- Browse the Marketplace for extensions that match your needs.

- Install and manage extensions seamlessly from within Visual Studio.

8. Advanced Debugging:

Dig deeper into debugging by utilizing features like conditional breakpoints, data tips, and watch windows. These tools provide insights into your code's behavior during runtime.

9. Unit Testing and Test Explorer:

Integrate unit testing into your development process using Visual Studio's built-in test framework. Write unit tests, execute them, and view the results in the Test Explorer window.

10. AI-Assisted Coding:

Visual Studio is incorporating AI-driven features like IntelliCode, which suggests code completions based on patterns and practices learned from millions of code repositories.

Conclusion:

As you progress in your coding journey, mastering these advanced features in Microsoft Visual Studio will elevate your productivity and proficiency. These tools and functionalities are designed to help you write better code, debug more efficiently, optimize performance, and collaborate seamlessly with your team. By exploring and incorporating these advanced features into your development workflow, you'll be well-equipped to tackle complex challenges and build high-quality software applications with confidence.

12.2. Learning Resources and Further Education

In the rapidly evolving landscape of software development, continuous learning is essential to stay updated with the latest technologies, tools, and best practices. This chapter explores various learning resources and avenues for further education that can help you expand your skills and excel in your coding journey.

1. Online Tutorials and Documentation:

The official Microsoft documentation and tutorials are invaluable resources for deepening your understanding of Visual Studio's advanced features. They cover a wide range of topics, from specific tools to comprehensive guides on building different types of applications. For instance, the "Learn" section on the Visual Studio website provides step-by-step tutorials, code samples, and documentation on various topics.

2. Online Courses:

Numerous online platforms offer courses on Visual Studio and advanced coding techniques. Platforms like Coursera, Udemy, and Pluralsight provide comprehensive courses taught by industry experts. These courses often include video lectures, quizzes, and hands-on coding exercises to reinforce your learning.

3. Microsoft Learn:

Microsoft Learn is a free platform that offers interactive, guided learning paths for various Microsoft technologies, including Visual Studio. These learning paths provide a structured approach to learning and are ideal for both beginners and experienced developers looking to expand their skills.

4. Community and Forums:

Engaging with the developer community can be highly beneficial. Websites like Stack Overflow, GitHub Discussions, and Dev.to allow you to ask questions, share knowledge, and learn from others' experiences. Active participation in discussions can provide insights into real-world challenges and solutions.

5. Books and Ebooks:

Consider exploring books and ebooks dedicated to advanced Visual Studio features and techniques. These resources often provide in-depth insights, case studies, and practical examples that can enhance your proficiency.

6. Coding Challenges and Hackathons:

Participating in coding challenges on platforms like LeetCode, HackerRank, and Codeforces can help you apply your skills to solve real-world coding problems. Additionally, joining hackathons or coding competitions can provide hands-on experience and opportunities to collaborate with other developers.

7. Microsoft Certification:

Earning a Microsoft certification in Visual Studio or related technologies can validate your expertise and enhance your credibility. Microsoft offers various certification paths, such as the "Microsoft Certified: Azure Developer Associate" or "Microsoft Certified: DevOps Engineer Expert."

8. Meetups and Conferences:

Attending local developer meetups and industry conferences can connect you with like-minded professionals and provide opportunities for networking and learning from experts. Many conferences feature workshops and sessions on advanced coding techniques and tools.

9. Blogs and Online Content:

Many experienced developers and Microsoft MVPs maintain blogs where they share insights, tips, and tutorials related to Visual Studio and coding best practices. Following these blogs can provide a steady stream of valuable information.

10. Experimentation and Personal Projects:

One of the most effective ways to learn is by doing. Challenge yourself with personal coding projects that incorporate advanced features of Visual Studio. By experimenting and building real applications, you'll gain practical experience and deepen your understanding.

Conclusion:

As you explore the advanced features of Microsoft Visual Studio, remember that learning is an ongoing journey. The resources mentioned in this chapter offer a variety of avenues to further your education and hone your coding skills. Embrace continuous learning, stay curious, and leverage these resources to stay at the forefront of software development and continue advancing in your coding career.

12.3. Future Trends in Coding and Development

The world of coding and software development is in a constant state of evolution, with new technologies, methodologies, and trends shaping the future of the industry. As you delve into the advanced features of Microsoft Visual Studio and expand your coding horizons, it's important to stay informed about the future trends that will influence the way you code and develop applications.

1. Artificial Intelligence and Machine Learning:

Artificial Intelligence (AI) and Machine Learning (ML) are transforming various industries, and the field of software development is no exception. Developers are increasingly incorporating AI and ML techniques to create intelligent and predictive applications. Visual Studio provides tools and frameworks that enable you to integrate AI and ML models into your projects seamlessly.

For example, you can use the Azure Machine Learning service to build, deploy, and manage machine learning models. Visual Studio's integration with Azure services allows you to easily incorporate AI capabilities into your applications, such as natural language processing, image recognition, and predictive analytics.

2. Cloud-Native Development:

The cloud has revolutionized the way applications are built, deployed, and scaled. Cloud-native development focuses on creating applications optimized for cloud environments. With Visual Studio and Azure, you can leverage cloud services, serverless computing, and containers to build scalable and resilient applications.

Visual Studio's integration with Azure Kubernetes Service (AKS) allows you to deploy and manage containerized applications with ease. This trend empowers developers to focus on writing code while the underlying infrastructure and scaling are managed by the cloud platform.

3. Low-Code and No-Code Development:

Low-code and no-code platforms are empowering individuals with limited coding experience to create applications through visual interfaces and pre-built components. Visual Studio is adapting to this trend by providing tools that enable rapid application development without extensive coding.

You can explore Power Apps within Visual Studio, which allows you to create custom apps with minimal coding. Additionally, Logic Apps enable you to automate workflows and integrate various services using a visual designer.

4. Internet of Things (IoT) Integration:

The IoT landscape is expanding rapidly, with devices becoming more interconnected and intelligent. Visual Studio offers features for building IoT applications and connecting devices to the cloud.

You can use Visual Studio to develop applications that collect, analyze, and act on data from IoT devices. With Azure IoT Hub integration, you can manage and monitor devices at scale, enabling scenarios such as remote monitoring and predictive maintenance.

5. Progressive Web Applications (PWAs):

PWAs combine the best of web and native applications, offering a responsive and engaging user experience. Visual Studio supports PWA development by providing tools for creating web applications that can be installed on users' devices and accessed offline.

By utilizing Visual Studio's capabilities, you can build PWAs that leverage service workers, push notifications, and other modern web features to deliver seamless user experiences across different devices and platforms.

6. Quantum Computing:

While still in its early stages, quantum computing holds the potential to revolutionize various fields, including cryptography, optimization, and scientific simulations. Visual Studio is positioning itself to support quantum development as this technology matures.

You can explore the Quantum Development Kit within Visual Studio, which provides a comprehensive environment for building and simulating quantum applications. While quantum computing is a complex and specialized field, Visual Studio's tools aim to make it more accessible to developers.

Conclusion:

As you embark on your journey to master the advanced features of Microsoft Visual Studio, keep a watchful eye on these future trends in coding and development. Embracing these trends will not only enhance your skills but also empower you to create innovative and impactful applications that shape the future of technology. By staying adaptable and open to learning, you'll be well-prepared to navigate the exciting challenges and opportunities that lie ahead in the dynamic world of coding.

CONCLUTION

In the ever-evolving landscape of coding and software development, Microsoft Visual Studio stands as a powerful and versatile tool that empowers developers to bring their ideas to life. Through the comprehensive journey we've embarked upon in this book, we hope you have gained a deep understanding of not only the fundamental concepts of coding but also the advanced features and techniques that Visual Studio offers.

Our goal in crafting this book was to provide you with a practical and hands-on guide that equips you with the skills and knowledge needed to thrive in the world of coding. From the basics of coding to the intricacies of working with libraries, building applications, testing APIs, collaborating with teams, and exploring emerging trends, we've covered a wide spectrum of topics to ensure you're well-prepared for the challenges and opportunities that lie ahead.

As you turn the final pages of this book, we extend our sincere gratitude to you, the reader. Your decision to invest your time and effort into mastering the art of coding with Microsoft Visual Studio is commendable and inspiring. We hope that the insights, examples, and guidance presented in these chapters have enriched your coding journey and broadened your horizons.

Remember, coding is not just about syntax and tools; it's about problem-solving, creativity, and continuous learning. With the knowledge gained from this book, we encourage you to embark on your coding projects with confidence, experiment with new ideas, and contribute to the ever-growing landscape of technology.

Thank you for choosing "Coding Basics with Microsoft Visual Studio." We believe that the skills you've acquired here will serve as a strong foundation for your future endeavors in coding and software development. As you navigate the exciting path ahead, may your passion for coding continue to drive you, and may your creations leave a lasting impact on the world.

Happy coding, and best wishes for your coding journey!